Read This First

Serving Two Masters With One Goal—Getting R⁺

"You can't serve two masters," goes the old sayⁱⁿ
Sure you can. This book is proof of that.
The two masters I served in this book arᵉ
Dream—the first dream is getting rich slo   ₐnd
the second, *getting rich fast* in four to five y
Whether you want to get rich fast or slow,   ₛame wealth-
building principles. I call these principles **gettiₙ   .ₐ.L.** because each
letter in the word **REAL** stands for one of the ₁our key principles that
rich people have used to get rich and stay rich for centuries—**Recurring
income... Equity... Appreciation...** and **Leverage**.

The first part of this book explains the **Museum Method™**, the name
I've coined to describe the slow and steady method of getting rich. I
dedicate a chapter to each of the four **R.E.A.L. principles** (Chapters 3, 4,
5, and 6) and give examples of how millions of people, myself included,
have used these principles to create financial freedom. If you follow the
advice in these chapters starting early in your working career, you're
almost guaranteed to become a millionaire before you retire.

In Chapter 7, I describe a hyper-dynamic business model that
compresses the **R.E.A.L. principles** into months and years, instead of
decades. I call this the **Modern Method™** because it's fast-paced and
fast-acting, perfect for the modern-day mentality.

I'll be the first to tell you that the **Modern Method™** I describe is not
the only way to get rich fast in four to five years. I know people who have
made a quick killing in commodities. People who have made millions
in e-commerce businesses. People who have pocketed a bundle building
houses. People who have struck it rich in the restaurant business. The list
goes on and on.

But when a restaurant fails or a franchise closes its doors or a real
estate investor can't cover his notes, things turn ugly quickly. I've seen
people lose millions of dollars in conventional businesses, and when that
happens, the losses snowball, and sometimes they end up losing their
savings. And their homes. And even their families. Not pretty.

That's why, in my opinion, the *low cost of entry and high-profit
potential* make the **Modern Method** the average person's best opportunity
to get rich... live rich... and retire rich. Tens of thousands of people are
using the **Modern Method** to **get R.E.A.L. and get rich**—and so can
you.

GET
R.E.A.L.*
& GET RICH!

Omar **P**eriu **I**nc.
International

R. E. A. L.
Acknowledgments

I wish to express my sincere gratitude to the wonderful people who have helped and inspired me to fulfill my dreams. Your encouragement and confidence keep me moving toward my mission to help others achieve greatness the way I was helped.

First, I would like to thank Dr. Stephen Price for your creative contributions toward this book. Your extraordinary skills, talent, and artistry are the reasons this book will help so many people.

Thank you, Katherine Glover! Without your brilliant vision, this book would not exist. You are a true inspiration for anyone wishing to make their dreams a reality!

I would like to acknowledge Debbie Cortes with deep appreciation for all of your contributions, most especially, your superb marketing efforts.

To Ryan Jordan, I don't know what I would do without you. Thank you for taking care of me and my business while I am on my mission to help others create a better life for themselves and their families.

And last but not least, I would like to thank my mentors. Thank you, Tom Murphy, for investing your life in my life so I could make all my dreams, and the dreams of everyone we touch come true. And to Zig Ziglar, Tom Hopkins, Jim Rohn and Bob Proctor—thank you for your friendship and continual support from the beginning.

Dedication

I dedicate this book to my wife, Helen; my daughter, Alexandra; and my son, Maxwell, for their inspiration and support in my pursuit of excellence. A special debt of gratitude goes to my parents for the love and guidance they have given me throughout my life. They are my true role models.

Contents

Getting Rich by Getting R.E.A.L.

Most of the truly wealthy in this country don't live in Beverly Hills or on Park Avenue—they live next door.
—from the bestseller *The Millionaire Next Door*

Get real!

At one time or another, we've either been on the receiving end of this expression or we've hurled it at someone who has just made a wildly unrealistic statement, such as one of these:

"When I win the lottery, I'll buy a sailboat and retire in the Caribbean."

Get real!

"Social Security will be enough for me to live on in retirement."

Get real!

"Maybe a great aunt I never knew I had will leave me her fortune."

Get real!

"My son is going to play professional baseball, so he will take care of me in my old age."

Get real!

"I took care of my kids for the first 20 years of their lives, so they will take care of me the last 20 years of mine."

Get real!

Get R.E.A.L. and Get Rich

If one of these statements describes your plan for the future, then indeed, you need to "get real" because these are totally unrealistic methods for achieving financial independence.

There is a way, however, to achieve financial independence by "getting real." It's a proven methodology that rich people have used for centuries to get rich... and stay rich!

North America is drowning in an ocean of wealth, yet most people only have droplets of assets.

But the "real" I'm talking about isn't just a word, it's also an acronym—**R.E.A.L.**—with each letter standing for the four immutable wealth-building principles that have empowered millions of people from all cultures in all ages to attain and maintain financial freedom.

Here are the four time-honored principles of wealth creation that have improved the lives of millions over the centuries... and which can do the same for you.

R = **Recurring Income**—*do the work once and get paid again and again*
E = **Equity**—*own businesses, real estate, investments, and assets*
A = **Appreciation**—*grow your assets over time*
L = **Leverage**—*profit from other people's time, efforts, or money*

As you will learn in the coming pages, these four timeless principles apply to every wealth-building endeavor ever created, including real estate... retailing... franchising... stocks and bonds... IRAs... 401(k)s... CDs... government bonds... municipal bonds... money market funds... mutual funds... annuities... Network Marketing organizations... small businesses... large businesses... giant corporations... and trust funds.

Who Has Wealth—and Why

North America is drowning in an ocean of wealth, yet most people only have droplets of assets because they let their wealth slip through their fingers. The average household in the U.S. earns more than $50,000 a year, yet, excluding home equity, *the typical household has a net worth of less than $15,000 and a savings rate of less than zero!* For people over 65, the situation is even worse. Take away their Social Security benefits, and more than 50% of our citizens over 65 would live in poverty.

> When it comes to wealth, it's not how much you make that counts, it's how much you keep.

A small percentage of people, however, have managed to maintain and even grow their wealth. Many of these people earn even less than the median household income of $50,000, but they have accumulated substantial wealth over their lifetimes, proving that when it comes to wealth, it's not how much you make that counts, *it's how much you keep (and how wisely you invest what you keep).*

We've all heard the expression "The rich get richer." Statistics bear this out. Nearly 50% of the wealth in North America is owned by only 3.5% of the households.

How did those lucky 3.5% get rich? Most people assume that to get rich, you have to inherit a ton of money... or win the lottery... or be super-smart... or super-lucky. But research shows that the vast majority of millionaires got wealthy because they *decided* to get rich, and then created and followed a plan that would make it happen. The vast majority of millionaires get rich by getting **R.E.A.L.**, that is, by consistently taking advantage of **Recurring income... Equity... Appreciation...** and **Leverage** over long periods of time. The authors of the mega-bestseller *The Millionaire Next Door* say it best:

> Research shows that the vast majority of millionaires got wealthy because they decided to get rich.

"It is seldom luck or inheritance or advanced degrees or even intelligence that enables people to amass fortunes. Wealth is more often the result of a lifestyle of hard work, perseverance, planning, and most of all, self-discipline."

Never a Better Time Than Right Here, Right Now

It's easy to forget that most North Americans are only three generations away from the Great Depression and only four generations away from dire poverty. Compared to previous generations, the average lifestyle today is grander than our ancestors could ever have imagined—and, unlike our great-grandparents, the majority of North Americans have the potential to amass wealth that will last a lifetime.

50% of the world's population—more than 3 BILLION people—exists on $2 a day or less.

Today, right now, we're living in the best time in history... in the best geographic area... and in the best economic system to create financial independence. American families have never earned more income, spent less on basic necessities, had a higher standard of living, or had more business opportunities, e.g., small businesses, franchising, consulting, and direct selling, than we do today. Just compare today's economic conditions to the early part of the 20th century:

A century ago, most jobs paid less than 30 cents per hour, and the average household earned $750 a year. Today, the average is $50,500.

A century ago, only 20% of families owned a home. Today, close to 70% of us own homes.

A century ago, Americans spent 80% of their income on the necessities of food, clothing, and housing. Today, we spend less than 50%.

A century ago, 40% of Americans worked on farms, mostly as low-paid day laborers. Today, 98% of us either work for ourselves or are employed in vocations unrelated to agriculture.

A century ago, life expectancy was 47 years. Today, it's 77.

A century ago, there were fewer than 10,000 cars in North

America being driven on a few hundred miles of paved roads. Today, there are 150 million passenger cars (plus another 100 million commercial vehicles) driving on 4 million miles of highways, roads, and streets.

Compared to previous generations, we've got it made in the shade. And compared to the rest of the world, where 50% of the world's population—more than 3 BILLION people—*exists on $2 a day or less,* we're richer than King Croesus.

> Today, becoming rich is a necessity, not just an option.

The Problem: Papa Pension Is Dying

I'm going to make a bold statement, but as you will soon see, the facts back me up. Here it is:

Today, becoming rich is a necessity, not just an option.

Why would I say such a thing? Because the funding for retirement is shifting from business and the federal government onto the shoulders of the workers themselves, which means if the average couple wants to maintain their standard of living during their retirement years, they're going to need to accumulate far more money than previous generations.

The root of the problem is that Papa Pension is dying, and once he's gone, the only person who can take care of you and your family is YOU! Like it or not (and most workers do NOT), we're in the midst of a new reality: Pensions are a thing of the past.

> Private pensions are going the way of the dodo bird.

"Private pensions are going the way of the dodo bird," says economist David Wyss. Statistics prove this out: In 1980, 84% of workers at medium and large companies enjoyed traditional pensions. Today, that figure is 21% and dropping like a stone.

The defined-benefit pension is an employee perk designed for a post-WWII world, a relatively brief period of high growth when American corporations were vying to attract and keep top talent. But the world has changed dramatically over the last 50 years, making pensions a luxury that companies, and even state and the federal governments, can no longer afford. Global competition... longer life expectancies... constant seismic changes in the marketplace... the massive Baby Boom population nearing retirement age... and soaring healthcare costs have all pounded nails in the coffin of Papa Pension.

As a result, younger Fortune 500 companies, such as Dell, Microsoft, and Starbucks, have ignored pensions from the start, while old-economy companies, such as GM and IBM, are freezing pensions or converting them into 401(k)s.

Why Workers Have to Get Real by "Getting R.E.A.L."

Now, here's the really scary part about living in the post-pension age. According to the Employee Benefit Research Institute, *even though only 21% of workers are enrolled in a defined-benefit plan, 61% expect to receive benefits from such a plan in retirement*!

In other words, 40% of workers are NOT enrolled in a pension plan and they don't even know it (or want to admit it). Talk about a disconnect! To complicate matters, Social Security starts going cash-flow negative somewhere around the year 2012.

It's time to get real!

"The real problems happen," says CPA and financial planner Drew Tignanelli, *"when people don't face the facts."*

> The number one financial concern among all working Americans was retirement (56%).

People are not only ignoring their looming financial problems, many are pretending those problems will magically morph into prosperity. Here are some sobering "heads-stuck-in-the-sand" statistics that indicate Americans are deep in denial about their financial futures:

- 40% of workers think they're entitled to pensions, even though their employer doesn't offer a pension plan.
- 75% of workers over age 40 say they're "somewhat confident" they'll have enough money for retirement, even though 31% of those same workers have not yet started saving money for retirement.
- 66% of workers do not have an IRA or similar retirement plan.

- 33% of workers are passing on their company's 401(k) plan, which means they're turning their backs on TAX-FREE MONEY their company is trying to GIVE them.

And I thought *Dumb and Dumber* was just the title of a movie.

Retirement on Everyone's Mind

You hear a lot these days about the tens of millions of aging Baby Boomers who are financially unprepared for retirement. Turns out the Boomers aren't the only ones worrying—*their children are worried also*! According to a recent American Retirement Study done by the online brokerage Scottrade, "The number one financial concern among all working Americans was retirement (56%)."

So, what are the Boomers' kids doing about it? Little more than worrying, it appears. According to the study, "71% of Americans age 35 to 44 admit they have not saved enough to retire at age 65." Yet—now here's the kicker—only 33% of the respondents have an IRA or similar retirement plan. Let's see, 71% think they don't have enough saved, but 40% of those aren't doing anything about it.

So, my question is this: Why, despite living in the wealthiest region of the world during the most prosperous period in our history, has the average family accumulated only $15,000 of assets (other than the equity in their homes) during their working years and why are so many Americans financially ill-prepared to face their "Golden Years"?

The short answer: Lack of knowledge about how wealth is accumulated and lack of discipline to save and invest wisely.

> Truth is, the average family makes plenty of money to become rich by retirement age.

What You Will Learn in This Book

Truth is, the average family makes plenty of money to become rich by retirement age, but they lack what I call the **Three Ds**—the **Do's**... the **Don'ts**... and the **Discipline**. In this book, I'll teach you the **Do's** and **Don'ts** to getting rich. As for the **Discipline** to follow through on my advice, well, that's up to you.

In the coming pages, you'll learn how average people—people like you and me—can get rich by employing the same **"Get R.E.A.L."™ strategies** that wealthy people have been using since the days of Solomon.

You'll learn how to *maximize returns* on your investments while minimizing risk.

You'll learn about the **BLISS formula™ for financial freedom** that, once implemented, can turn a portion of your monthly earnings into permanent assets that will make your retirement years blissful, indeed.

> The Modern Method is the Museum Method juiced up on steroids.

You'll learn about a wealth-building concept called **compounding**—a mathematical concept so powerful that Einstein called it "the eighth wonder of the world"—and why it's every millionaire's key investment strategy.

You'll learn about the **ABCD plan™** for getting rich, a four-step plan that virtually guarantees you'll become rich by retirement.

You'll learn tips about buying, selling, and holding stocks, bonds, and real estate, plus the advantages (and disadvantages) of owning franchises and small businesses.

You'll learn about the difference between the **real work** you do at your day job... and **R.E.A.L. work™** you perform evenings and weekends.

You'll learn about slow and steady wealth-building strategies I call the **Museum Method™** because they're classic and artful, and have worked for centuries.

You'll learn about something I call the **Modern Method™**, a dynamic hybrid business model better known as Network Marketing. The **Modern Method** is the **Museum Method** juiced up on steroids, a low-cost, potentially high-profit opportunity that's enabling thousands of people to create wealth in months and years, instead of decades.

And finally, I'll introduce you to the **Millionaire Mentality™**, a positive, prosperity-oriented mindset that will keep you thinking like a millionaire until you become one.

Back from the Edge of the Cliff

"Live for today, plan for tomorrow," says my friend Burke Hedges. Well, Americans are great at living for today... for right now... for instant gratification. *But most of us are terrible at planning for tomorrow.*

But what happens to those who don't plan ahead? To answer that, I'm going to tell you a true story about the tragic consequences of "falling" for an illusion. Here's the story:

There's an outcropping of granite that rises nearly 1,000 feet above the Georgia plains surrounding Atlanta. The massive rock, called Stone Mountain, is rounded and is nearly five miles in circumference. Today, Stone Mountain is home to a popular amusement park, but back in earlier times, visitors would climb to the top and start walking to what appeared to be the edge of a cliff.

> Apply the principles of R.E.A.L. in your life and you can become a real card-carrying member of the Millionaires' Club

But because the rock was gently rounded over several miles, there was no perceivable edge, only an ever-receding illusion of an edge. Occasionally, people would walk too far toward the horizon. When they finally turned around to go back, they'd realize too late they had ventured too far, and, unable to keep their footing on the steep slope, they'd fall to their deaths.

Not Too Late to Get R.E.A.L. and Get Rich

I see a similar thing happening to millions of Americans as they stroll through their daily lives unconcerned about their financial future until it's too late.

News flash. Like Stone Mountain, once you pass a certain point, there ain't no goin' back.

Fortunately, it's not too late for you. In the coming pages, I'll give you a full understanding of how to Get Rich by Getting R.E.A.L. I promise that by the end of this book you'll understand how the R.E.A.L. principles have worked for others… and how they can work for you.

But understanding is only step one.

Action is step two.

We've all heard that knowledge is power. Well, I say knowledge isn't power. I say, *Knowledge **put to use** is power!*

This book will give you the knowledge that rich people have used for thousands of years to get rich and stay rich. Once you've acquired that knowledge, it's up to you to put it into practice.

Apply the principles of R.E.A.L. in your life and you can become a *real* card-carrying member of the Millionaires' Club.

I look forward to welcoming you to the club.

Overview: Why Get R.E.A.L.?

A workplace revolution is under way. No sensible
person expects to spend a lifetime in a single
corporation anymore. Some call this shift the
"end of corporate responsibility." I call it... "The
Beginning of Renewed Individual Responsibility."
—Tom Peters
management guru

Bling.

That's the word teens use to describe the flashy jewelry that the rappers and professional athletes wear to impress their adoring fans. Supposedly, bling is the "sound" of light reflecting off a diamond. *Bling!*

All too often, the newfound wealth of young celebrities doesn't last much longer than the sound—*bling!*

Case in point: Mike Tyson, former heavyweight boxing champion, earned more than $300 million in the ring and millions more in endorsements during the 1980s and '90s. Tyson was heavy into the bling thing. He owned Rolls-Royces and diamond rings and Rolex watches.

In August of 2003, Iron Mike filed for bankruptcy.

Bling today, gone tomorrow.

What Is the Key to Getting Rich?

The key to getting rich and staying rich isn't to make more money. There are plenty of people who make tons of money but live paycheck to paycheck. As Robert Kiyosaki and Donald Trump write in their latest bestseller, *Why We Want You to Be Rich*, "We believe you cannot solve money problems with money. You can only solve money problems with financial education."

> **You cannot solve money problems with money. You can only solve money problems with financial education.**

Okay—I know what you're thinking: "You can't solve money problems with money. What kind of nonsense is that? More money is the only way to solve money problems."

Not so.

Unless you have the self-discipline to save your money and the know-how to make it grow, millions can slip through your fingers like a spring breeze through a screen door.

To prove my point, all you have to do is look what happens to lottery winners who get a sudden windfall of money but lack financial knowledge and personal discipline.

- **Evelyn Adams** won the New Jersey lottery not just once, but twice, for a total of $5.4 million. Today, she's broke and lives in a trailer.
- **Bud Post** won $16.2 million in the 1988 Pennsylvania lottery. Within a year, he was $1 million in debt. He declared bankruptcy and now lives on Social Security.
- **Suzanne Mullins** won $4.2 million in 1993. Now she's deeply in debt to a company that lent her money using the winnings as collateral. Her lawyer says she has zero assets.
- **Ken Proxmire**, a machinist, won $1 million in the Michigan lottery. Within five years, he filed for bankruptcy. Today, he's back working as a machinist.
- **Charles Riddle** of Belleville, Michigan, won $1 million in 1975. Soon afterward, he was broke and indicted for selling cocaine.

- **Willie Hurt** won $3.1 million in 1989. He got divorced and took a liking to crack cocaine. Two years later, he was broke and tried for murder.
- **Janite Lee** won $18 million in 1993. Eight years later, he filed for bankruptcy with only $700 in two bank accounts and no cash on hand.

I know, you're likely thinking, "Those people were idiots. No way I'd let millions slip through my fingers." But sadly, most people DO let millions slip through their fingers.

The facts tell an all-too-common tale:

The average family in the U.S. earns $50,000 a year before taxes. Assuming they earn that money from age 25 until they retire at 65, the typical family would earn $2 million dollars total. *Yet, other than their homes, the net worth of the average household is less than $15,000!*

What happened to those millions? Like the lottery winners, it just somehow disappeared for a lack of financial education and discipline. The facts tell the tale of misspent money and missed opportunities to create lasting wealth— and not just for some loony lottery winners, but also for half the families in North America.

> The typical family would earn $2 million dollars total. Yet, other than their homes, the net worth of the average household is less than $15,000!

What about you? Are you letting financial freedom slip through your fingers one shopping spree at a time? If so, it's not too late to get back on track to **getting rich... by getting R.E.A.L.**

True Meaning of the Word "Rich"

Most people equate being rich with living a grand lifestyle—big home, several expensive foreign cars, country club memberships, glamorous vacations, fancy furnishings, and so on. The bling thing.

But ostentatious consumption is not the same as being rich. The authors of *The Millionaire Next Door* say it best:

"Wealth is not the same as income. If you make a good income each year and spend it all, you are not getting wealthier. You are just living high. Wealth is what you accumulate, not what you spend."

That last sentence is worth repeating—*"Wealth is what you accumulate, not what you spend."* My sentiments exactly. When I use the word "rich" in this book, I'm not talking about the shallow, short-term bling effect. I'm more interested in the lasting, long-term ramifications of being rich, which means getting rich and staying rich so that you can do what you want… when you want… with whom you want. What could be better than that?

The word rich didn't start out being about bling. Just the opposite, in fact. Rich is a derivation of the Latin *rex*, which translates to "king"; and the Sanskrit *raj*, meaning "to rule."

Those definitions are just as applicable today as they were thousands of years ago because truly rich people are the kings and queens of their own castles with the power to make their own decisions… the power to set their own agendas… and the power to rule their own lives.

The Dollar Definition of Rich

Just so there's no confusion about what I mean when I use the word rich, I'm going to give you my concrete, measurable definition.

Omar's Dollar Definition of Rich: *Rich is having a net worth of a million dollars or more in assets other than your home.*

If you've reached the million-dollar plateau, in my book, you're rich so long as you maintain that million-dollar asset level. Start whittling away at your million-dollar nest egg by cashing in your assets to buy depreciable liabilities, like expensive new cars and luxury vacations for the entire family, and you run the risk of falling into the consumer trap of living high.

My reasoning for choosing the million-dollar threshold is twofold:

One, it's realistic and easily doable for the typical household to accumulate $1 million during their working years by understanding and applying the principles in this book.

And two, having at least $1 million in liquid assets will ensure that the average household will be able to retire with the same annual income (or more) without spending a dime of their $1 million nest egg!

How can they do that? Simple. Let's do the math.

> Rich is having a net worth of a million dollars or more in assets other than your home.

Million-Dollar Math

Let's assume that "the Smiths," a long-married couple, are average income earners. They make $50,000 a year and own the average home valued at $220,000. Over the years, the Smiths have saved monthly, and because they have taken full advantage of tax-deferred IRAs and 401(k)s, as well as investing in two rental properties, they have accumulated $1 million in total assets other than their home.

The Smiths decide to retire at 65. To make sure their assets last their lifetimes, they sell all of their assets and buy CDs paying 4% a year in interest, which is near the historical average for short-term income investments. Multiply 4% times $1 million, and you get $40,000 a year income. Assuming one or both spouses receives only $1,000 a month in Social Security, the Smiths would earn $52,000 a year without spending so much as a penny of their $1 million nest egg. So, when they both pass away in their late 80s, they can pass on their $1 million in assets (plus the value of their home along with any life insurance they carry) to their children or charity or church.

That's rich.

That's powerful.

And that's doable.

How doable? We'll start getting into the specifics of how to build a nest egg of $1 million in Chapter 5, but first, let's step back and look at a master plan for creating financial freedom that I call the **BLISS formula**.

BLISS Formula for Financial Freedom

We're all creatures of habits, and our habits shape every aspect of our lives. We have work habits. Eating habits. Exercise habits.

Morning habits. Evening habits. Sleeping habits. And spending habits. Show me a person with positive, healthy habits, and I'll show you a happy, healthy individual.

Surveys show that the average person spends more time planning a vacation than planning their financial future.

In this book, we're going to concentrate on creating positive, healthy financial habits. To **get rich by getting R.E.A.L.**, you need to adopt a program of healthy habits that I call the **BLISS formula for financial freedom**.

The word "bliss" means a state of great joy or happiness. One of the ways to achieve bliss in your life is to eliminate financial worries, especially in your retirement years. The **BLISS formula** can help you do just that. **BLISS** is another acronym (love those acronyms 'cause they're great memory aids) for the actions you need to take to create financial independence.

Here's what each letter in the BLISS formula stands for:

Budget   Learn   Invest   Save   Spend

Let's take a few moments to discuss each of these key habits and how they impact your ability to get rich.

B – Budget: A budget is a monthly money management plan for your household. Budgets are easy to set up, but hard for some people to follow. The first place to start is to go through your cancelled checks and credit card statements to see what you spend money on each month. There are dozens of great budgeting tips and plans available for free online. Just google "create a budget" and choose among the dozens of websites.

L – Learn: Surveys show that the average person spends more time planning a vacation than planning their financial future. To *have* what rich people have, you must *do* what rich people do. And what rich people *do* is learn how to get money and keep money. So start LEARNING what rich people do by reading books, listening to mentors, and seeking money-making opportunities.

I – Invest: *Average people work for money* and have little to show for it at the end of their careers. *Rich people make their money work for them* by investing their time, efforts, and money-building networks and in growing their assets via the stock market and real estate.

S – Save: Rich people pay themselves first by saving AT LEAST 10-20% of their gross income and then investing it wisely.

S – Spend: Rich people Budget... Learn... Invest... and Save BEFORE THEY SPEND, while middle class and poor people ignore the first four letters of the BLISS formula and skip right to the fifth letter—SPEND! Never forget: The true measure of rich is how much you accumulate, not how much you spend.

> Average people work for money. Rich people make their money work for them.

There's a Method to Becoming a Millionaire

According to a report by the investment bank Merrill Lynch, there are 8.7 million MILLIONAIRES in the world today. That's a LOT of millionaires, don't you think? But considering the world population is more than 6.5 BILLION, only about one out of every 1,000 people becomes a member of the "Millionaires' Club."

So, how did MOST of these millionaires get rich? By getting R.E.A.L., that's how... by taking advantage of business opportunities and by investing in financial instruments that take advantage of R.E.A.L. wealth-building principles: **Recurring Income... Equity... Appreciation...** and **Leverage**.

The simple truth is, for most couples in North America, getting rich is a matter of choice.

> For most couples in North America, getting rich is a matter of choice.

Getting rich means choosing to save when you're tempted to spend.

Getting rich means forgoing short-term "bling" in favor of long-term wealth accumulation.

Getting rich means following the **BLISS formula for financial freedom**.

Getting rich means being open to unconventional opportunities, like Network Marketing, that conventional people turn their backs on.

Getting rich means adopting a **Millionaire Mentality** that keeps you focused on your dream and believing in yourself.

Getting rich means, most of all, MAKING IT HAPPEN, not just wishing it would happen.

For Things to Change, You Have to Change

Here's an old joke about what happens when people refuse to change:

Two old college buddies spend an evening together in a bar. They have such a great time that they vow to meet again at the same bar, same time, 10 years from now.

Ten years later, the first guy walks in and squints through the dark room looking for his friend. Sure enough, there's his good buddy sitting on the same barstool he was sitting on 10 years before.

"Hey, pal, great to see you again," he shouts, patting his buddy on the back. "Have to admit, though, I really didn't expect to see you again after we left that night."

The friend at the bar looks up through bloodshot eyes, sways slightly, and slurs, "Who left?"

To Get Ahead, You Gotta Get Off Your "Barstool"

We laugh at the punch line, but the story saddens us, too, because we all know people like the guy on the barstool, the people who are wedded to bad habits that hold them back from realizing their full potential.

In this story, the bad habit was drinking. But the bad habit could just as easily be eating poorly. Or staying in a job you hate. Or spending more money than you make.

To **get rich by getting R.E.A.L.**, you've gotta get off your mental "barstool" because if you're not well on your way to creating financial independence, then you're stuck in the same rut as the guy in the story.

Look, I'm not telling you to do anything I didn't have to do. In the mid-1980s, I was stuck in a rut living paycheck to paycheck, just like most Americans.

But I made the decision to get out of the paycheck parade and get rich.

To read my story about how a college dropout went from minimum wage to a multi-millionaire, turn to the next chapter.

Chapter 2

My Story: From Minimum Wage to Multi-Millionaire

Don't knock the rich. When was the last time you were hired by somebody poor?

—Robert Orben
author and magician

Back in the late-1970s, when I was working in a stone quarry for minimum wage, I remember feeling two jaw-clenching emotions—boredom and anger.

Boredom because my job—cleaning and greasing the pulleys on the giant buckets hauling blasted rock to the surface—was tedious and repetitive and mind numbing. And anger because I was working 10-12 hours a day, caked with sweat and dust, dreaming of a singing career but destined (or so it seemed at the time) to spend my life waist deep in water 30 feet underground doing menial labor for minimum wage.

The work was backbreaking.

But I was strong.

And my dream was even stronger.

After a year and a half, I saved enough money to pursue my dream of becoming a recording artist. I rented a U-Haul trailer, loaded up all my belongings, and headed to California. Six days later, tired and hungry, I steered my dented Pontiac GTO belching smoke (but minus the trailer, which tumbled down a ravine somewhere on the western slope of the Rockies) into the outskirts of Los Angeles.

I thought I was on my way to fame and fortune as a singer.

Record producers thought otherwise. I got turned down by every record company in L.A.

Broke and discouraged, I took a job as a personal trainer at a health club in Los Angeles (earning minimum wage, of course) and moved into a 200-square-foot apartment. The weather and working conditions were nicer than the quarry, but minimum wage was minimum wage, and I struggled to make ends meet. The owner suggested I try sales because "that's where the real money is."

For me, at that time, sales was where the money was *not*. My first nine months, I earned $147 a month working on commission only. I was dead last on the sales team. I had finally hit the ultimate bottom—*I was earning LESS than minimum wage!*

A Mentor Enters My Life

Just when I thought things would never improve, I met Tom Murphy. Murphy was one of the investors in the health club and a partner of Tom Hopkins, America's leading sales trainer. I asked Murphy for help, and he suggested I enroll in a weekend sales seminar he had organized.

> Looking rich isn't the same as being rich. If you want to be rich, you have to change your thinking habits and spending habits

"You pay for the event, and I'll give you free copies of all the speakers' tapes and books," he said. I jumped at his offer. After immersing myself in the material, I began to see immediate improvements in my sales job. One year after attending the seminar, I went from the worst sales person to number one.

Before long, I was promoted to general manager of all 28 clubs in the L.A. area. As G.M., I earned a salary plus an override on all sales if I met my quota. For the first time in my life, I was off the minimum wage merry-go-round. I was only 25 years old and earning major money.

So, what did I do with my newfound wealth? I spent it. A buddy and I had a race to see who could collect the most credit cards. I won by accumulating 17. I bought a brand new Mercedes. Ate in five-star restaurants. Bought a Rolex and handmade suits. By the time I was in my late 20s, I looked like a million bucks, but I was carrying $67,000 in credit card debt. A conversation with Murphy set me on the right path to getting real... and getting rich.

"How much money you got in the bank?" Murphy asked one evening as I complained to him about my inability to get ahead.

"None," I replied.

"Big hat, no cattle," he quipped.

"What's that supposed to mean?" I asked.

"Means lots of flash, but no cash. Means you're more interested in appearances than principles. Looking rich isn't the same as being rich. You *look* rich but don't have a dime in the bank. If you want to *be* rich, you have to change your thinking habits and spending habits. That's it in a nutshell."

The more Murphy talked, the more I realized that by trying to look rich, I was repeating the spending habits of my father, who had made and lost two fortunes by the time he was 47. He'd also suffered two heart attacks by that age. So, I made the *decision* to do what rich people do so I could *be* rich, not just look the part.

> Anybody with average intelligence and a burning desire can become rich in this country.

I was on my way.

The Back Story of My Journey from Minimum Wage to Millionaire

Before I tell you how I made my first million, I want to take you back to my childhood to show you that anybody with average intelligence and a burning desire can become rich in this country, no matter how humble their background.

I'm living proof of that statement.

Here's my story.

I was born into a wealthy Cuban family. I was the youngest of four children, three boys and a girl. My dad owned several ESSO gas stations and a Mercury/Lincoln dealership outside of Camaquey, Cuba. We lived in a mansion attended by cooks, maids, and butlers.

On New Year's Day, 1959, all of that changed. Castro took over the country, and during the ensuing years, he confiscated all private property and executed or imprisoned all opposition. Because my father was a successful capitalist, he knew his days were numbered. So, in 1961, he spent all but his last $200 in arranging to fly the family to Miami, where we stayed in a one-room apartment in Little Havana courtesy of the U.S. government until arrangements could be made with a church to help us out.

> The adjustments to my new home were tough, but, as we all know, the toughest lessons are the best lessons.

Three months later, St. Patrick's in Joliet, Illinois, sponsored us. We flew to the Midwest in the dead of winter, arriving in Joliet during a blizzard with a foot of snow on the ground. I was 7 years old, had never seen snow, owned only the clothes on my back, and didn't speak a word of English.

Needless to say, we experienced big-time culture shock!

Our clothes were hand-me-downs from the Salvation Army, and I remember our first meal being served in a galvanized bucket. We were the only Hispanic family in Joliet, and, because of my small size and inability to speak English, I was placed back a year in school.

Few days went by when my brothers and I didn't end up in a fight on the playground. I was small but athletic, and after holding my own against the toughest guy in school, he became my best friend and English tutor, teaching me one new word of English each day.

The adjustments to my new home were tough, but, as we all know, the toughest lessons are the best lessons, and because I was struggling to learn a new language, I learned to focus intently and listen carefully, skills that have served me well over the years.

Dad Earns Back His "Fortune"

While my siblings and I were struggling in school, my dad found work as a mechanic. He was smart and ambitious, and for him, working as a mechanic was a starting point, not a career move. My father eventually opened his own 10-stall garage, and when the money started coming in, he started buying property. Within nine years, the man who came to this country with a wife, four kids, and only the clothes on his back owned an auto repair shop, an auto parts store, three gas stations, and all of the houses on our block.

Unfortunately, my dad's appetite for investing was undermined by his even bigger appetite for spending. He never forgot his days as an "aristocrat" in Cuba, and he frittered away his assets by buying new luxury cars and hand-tailored suits, just as I was to do 10 years later. Over-extended in real estate (and over-spending on status items to impress the neighbors), my father put himself under enormous stress, culminating in the first of several heart attacks.

His house of cards started falling, and, in 1973, 12 years after moving to the U.S., my father lost everything for the second time.

Lessons from My Father

Flash forward to the 1980s. As so often happens, the son repeats the sins of the father—I was spending my money faster than I was earning it.

Remember the **BLISS formula** we discussed in the previous chapter? **BLISS** represents *millionaire habits*—**Budget... Learn... Invest... Save... Spend**. Like most Americans, I ignored the first four letters and raced right to the last **S—Spend**.

> BLISS represents millionaire habits— Budget... Learn... Invest... Save... Spend.

Although older and supposedly wiser, my dad also had a spending habit. He understood the principles of investing, which enabled him to accumulate businesses and real estate, but because he budgeted poorly and always spent more than he earned, it was just a matter of time before his house of cards came tumbling down.

Before I met Murphy, I was headed down the same road. But Murphy opened my eyes to the realities of getting rich. And, to my credit, I was eager to learn, and I pumped him for every bit of information I could get. With Murphy's help, I put together a plan to get rich. The plan worked. By making a **budget** and sticking to it... **learning** about business principles and how to operate health clubs profitably... **investing** in health clubs and real estate... **saving** 50% of my net income... and **spending** far less than I earned, I was able to go from $67,000 in debt to being a multi-millionaire in five years.

> One of the first things Murphy taught me was the importance of owning businesses, rather than just working for someone else.

One of the first things Murphy taught me was the *importance of owning businesses*, rather than just working for someone else (we'll talk about this more in the coming chapters). I knew that fitness clubs were cash cows, so I asked Murphy how I could get into an ownership position. He said I could become part owner of a new club for $20,000, a bargain, he assured me.

One problem. I was deep in debt and had no savings. How was I going to get $20,000 to invest? Rather than make excuses, I started asking guys in the club what they did for a living, hoping to hit on a quick way to make some cash. There was a lot of construction going on in California at that time, so I scraped together the money to buy a paint compressor and started bidding on painting jobs.

How I Turned a $200 Compressor into $20 Million

My money-making plan was simple. I'd bid $100 below the lowest bid to get the job. I'd spray the walls and then hire some of my weight-lifting buddies to paint the trim for $6 an hour. This way I could knock out five to six apartments a night. Within six months, I'd saved $20,000 and invested in a health club along with Murphy. Then I sold my painting business to one of my buddies for $10,000 and set the money aside for the next investment.

Over the next five years, I was able to buy nine fitness clubs in

California. Once I built up the memberships, buyers would stream in the doors with offers. Over time, I sold all of the clubs, but with three of the clubs, I wisely retained ownership of the land, leasing it back to the owners, which guaranteed me a **recurring stream of income** that I could use for other investments.

Meanwhile, I started saving money and I stopped using my credit cards. Within two years, I paid off all my credit cards and haven't carried a balance since that time, more than 20 years ago. For the next decade, I saved and invested in real estate. I'd buy run-down places in good neighborhoods, fix them up, and then put them back on the market. Whatever profits I made I'd put back into future projects. From time to time, when I bought a property for a great price, I'd rent it out and use the tenant's money to pay the mortgage.

To date, I have bought and sold over 100 properties, and at one time I owned $20 million worth of real estate in three states—single-family homes, multi-units, commercial property, and vacant land.

To this day, I tell people that a $200 compressor is the best investment I ever made.

American Dream Can Be Your Reality

I tell you my story not to brag but to prove that you don't have to be born brilliant or come from money to become rich in North America. The American Dream is still alive and well. In fact, it's healthier than it has ever been because there are more money-making opportunities than ever before.

My big opportunities happened to be health clubs and real estate, but they could have just as easily been a thousand other opportunities floating around. As my friend, Dr. Steve Price, is fond of saying, *"Opportunities can fall in your lap... if you put your lap where opportunities fall."*

> People will find what they're looking for. If you're looking for an opportunity, that's what you'll find.

In the 1980s, health clubs and real estate fell into my lap. A decade later it was sales training. Tomorrow—who knows what will fall into my lap. The key is to have an open mind... and a soft lap.

In other words, people will find what they're looking for. If you're looking for an opportunity, that's what you'll find.

If you're looking for a minimum-wage job, that's what you'll find.

If you're looking for a paycheck every two weeks, that's what you'll find.

But if you're looking for opportunities to **get R.E.A.L. and get rich**, that's what you'll find.

If you're fortunate enough to live and work in North America, you've got a leg up on the rest of the world as far as your opportunities to get rich.

That's not an opinion. That's a fact.

Together, the U.S. and Canada make up *less than 5% of the world's population, yet we're home to 33% of the world's millionaires.* And the number of millionaire households is expected to double in the coming decade.

No question, if you're looking to get rich and if you live in North America, you're in the right place at the right time. I was looking to get rich, and I found a way, and I've met dozens of other millionaires who did the same. I had no business background when I got started in health clubs. I didn't inherit a fortune. I've never bought a lottery ticket, much less won a lottery. But I managed to capture my version of the American Dream by **getting R.E.A.L. and getting rich**—and so can you.

Another Day, Another Way

I leveraged real estate to create much of my wealth, and in the coming chapters, you'll learn how you can do the same. But real estate, like stocks and bonds, goes in cycles, and right now real estate prices are sky high in much of the country. Which means the best deals in real estate are likely years down the road.

Fortunately, there's another way to **get R.E.A.L. and get rich...** a proven system that has been around for 100 years and is one of the fastest-growing industries in the world.

It's a franchise-like system of distribution called Network Marketing.

This dynamic wealth-building system doesn't require any specialized education. And, best of all, the initial investment requires a few hundred dollars, tops, compared to the thousands of dollars (or more) to buy real estate and the hundreds of thousands of dollars to buy a big-name franchise.

But before I tell you how Network Marketing works and why it's the average person's last best chance to get rich, I'm going to tell you about the key principles of wealth creation, which are **Recurring income, Equity, Appreciation**, and **Leverage**. Then I'll show you how Network Marketing exploits each of these principles to create wealth at warp speed.

Turn the page to learn about the first key principle of wealth creation—**Recurring income**.

Chapter 3

Recurring Income: Building Pipelines

If you want to get rich, just find someone making lots of money and do what he's doing.

—J. Paul Getty
billionaire businessman

"Who are you—a bucket carrier? Or a pipeline builder?"

That's a question Burke Hedges poses early in his bestselling book *The Parable of the Pipeline.*

The Parable of the Pipeline tells the story of two hard-working cousins, Pablo and Bruno, who live in a small Italian village in the early 1800s. The village hires the cousins to carry water from a nearby river to a cistern in the town square. The work pays well, but it's backbreaking, so Pablo decides to build a pipeline in his spare time while Bruno continues to carry buckets.

In the short run, Bruno comes out ahead. But once Pablo gets his pipeline built, he doesn't have to carry buckets anymore. The water flows whether he works or not. It flows while he eats. It flows while he sleeps. It flows on the weekends while he plays. The more water that flows into the village, the more money that flows into Pablo's pockets.

Real Work vs. R.E.A.L. Work

The point of the parable is that **bucket carriers** trade their time for money, only getting paid when they show up and do the work. For bucket carriers, one hour of work equals one hour of pay. Extra pay requires extra work. And no work (due to illness or retirement) means no pay.

Pipeline builders, on the other hand, do the work once and get paid again and again. That's called **Recurring income**. Sure, pipeline builders have to maintain their pipelines to keep the recurring income flowing. But **Recurring income** frees up much of your time so you can build other pipelines.

> Bucket carriers trade their time for money. Pipeline builders, on the other hand, do the work once and get paid again and again.

Most people are bucket carriers. **Bucket carriers** are doing what I call **real work**, as opposed to **R.E.A.L. work**. **Real work** is the day-to-day labor that employees must perform to receive their bi-weekly paychecks. **Real work** is usually nine-to-five work, and in exchange for their paycheck, people doing real work are employed with one main goal in mind—*to build pipelines for the owners of the company.*

Think about that statement for a moment—*the main goal of people doing **real work** is to build pipelines of recurring income for the owners!* You see, owners of self-sustaining businesses have pipelines of **Recurring income**. Yes, owners need to manage employees and watch the store—that's part of maintaining the pipeline. But many businesses—such as successful franchises, large Network Marketing organizations, or rental properties that employ property managers— are **pipelines** that require little day-to-day labor on the part of the owner.

I call the work that owners do **R.E.A.L. work**. **R.E.A.L. work** gives you a pipeline of income that can make you rich by taking advantage of **Recurring income... Equity... Appreciation...** and **Leverage**.

That's one of the big reasons I started investing in rental properties years ago. If you buy an investment property in the right location for the right price, the income will cover your costs with some profit left over—with the added advantage of the renter paying your mortgage. Owning rental property with a positive cash flow is like having *people pay you* for the right to build *your* pipeline.

> Real work is usually nine-to-five work in exchange for a paycheck. R.E.A.L. work gives you a pipeline of income that can make you rich.

Doesn't get any better than that, does it?

Your Two Jobs: Real Work and R.E.A.L. Work

One of life's great ironies is that people will work hard eight to 10 hours a day, five to six days a week, building their employer's pipeline, but will do little or nothing during the evenings and weekends to build their own pipelines.

What's wrong with this picture?

Let me level with you—in the 1950s and '60s, when American manufacturing was in its heyday and company pensions were plush and plentiful, employees in corporate America could afford to let their employers build their pipelines for them.

Those days are over. Today, if you're wise, you'll work two jobs—a *day job carrying buckets…* and an *evening and weekend job building pipelines*. You work hard at your *day job*. You take pride in it. And you earn income that supports your family and your lifestyle.

But if you're a **bucket carrier**, no matter how much money you make, you need to become a **pipeline builder** to get rich and stay rich. Even the highest-paid bucket carriers, like high-priced attorneys or highly respected surgeons, never become rich until they build pipelines of recurring income that keep pumping out revenue even when they're not in the courtroom or operating room.

Most people are good at their day jobs and deserve the money they earn, but they're *real slackers at the evening jobs* of building pipelines. Think I'm exaggerating? The facts bear me out.

One of life's great ironies is that people will work hard eight to 10 hours a day, five to six days a week, building their employer's pipeline, but will do little or nothing during the evenings and weekends to build their own pipelines.

Cruising on the 'Titanic'

Federal Reserve data shows that's today's retirees get 90% of their income from Social Security and corporate pensions. So far, so good. But because pensions are drying up and Social Security is becoming increasingly over-burdened, tomorrow's retirees are going to have to build their own pension pipelines.

That's the **new reality**, whether you like it or not.

Unfortunately, the vast majority of the next generation of retirees is ignoring the **new reality**.

Instead of spending their free time building pipelines for the future, they're spending their money on depreciating items, like cars and flat-screen TVs, or expensive indulgences, such as 10-day cruises for the whole family. Big spenders are usually small savers, and they're cruising, all right—cruising on the *Titanic*, and each year the giant icebergs on the horizon get closer and closer.

The statistics tell the tale: Nearly 50% of workers 55 and older have less than $50,000 invested for retirement. For people who have a history of spending all they earn, $50,000 might last them a couple of years in retirement—tops. *Low savings (in 2006, the savings rate in the U.S. was less than zero, a negative 1%) and few if any investments—that's the first iceberg.*

The second iceberg is diminishing home equity. Traditionally, the biggest part of most American's net worth is tied up in our homes. Problem is, beginning in the early party-hearty 1990s, homeowners started treating their homes like piggy banks, taking out home equity loans at record rates to spend on non-essentials, like new cars and, yep, those cruises and trips to Disney.

Even senior citizens are getting caught up in the spending spree. Among workers 55 and older, almost 50% doubted they could pay off their mortgages before they retire, meaning one of every two retirees living on fixed incomes will still be making mortgage payments.

The third iceberg is an American epidemic—credit card debt. The average U.S. household carries a monthly balance of nearly $10,000 in credit card debt at 16% to 28% interest, meaning they're obligated to pay the credit card company a minimum of $1,600 a year in interest, year in and year out. Contrary to what most card holders think, credit card companies love it when customers miss payments because, in addition to raising interest rates to 28%, card issuers can charge stiff penalty fees, which account for 33% of the industry's revenue.

> The way to avoid catastrophe is to follow all of the letters in the BLISS formula.

As credit card debt rises, more and more cardholders pay just the monthly minimum, which just adds ether to the *Titanic's* fuel supply.

The chart below tells the tale.

Minimum Credit Card Payment Schedule
The cost, in years and dollars, of paying the minimum 2% on credit cards charging 17% annual interest

Balance	Total Cost	Total Time
$1,000	$2,590.35	17 years, 3 months
$2,500	$7,733.49	30 years, 3 months
$5,000	$16,305.34	40 years, 2 months

Man the Lifeboats by Getting R.E.A.L.

Okay, we've talked about three dreamboat-sinking icebergs looming on the horizon, threatening to turn North Americans' happy-go-lucky lifestyles into a shipwreck.

The good news is *you* don't have to go down with the ship. The way to avoid catastrophe is to follow all of the letters in the **BLISS** formula—**Budget... Learn... Invest... Save... Spend.** Most Americans get in trouble because they skip the first four letters (which require discipline and deferred gratification) and zip right to the last S—**Spend.**

Budget
Learn
Invest
Save
Spend

News flash—there are no shortcuts on the road to financial independence. Getting rich in America is more a matter of *want to* than *how to*. There are dozens of ways to create wealth, so if your *want to* is strong enough, you'll find your *how to*. Here is a partial list of investments that can help you get rich... and stay rich.

Home equity... stocks and bonds... real estate... money markets... unimproved land... commodities... 401(k)s... IRAs... secured loans... CDs... treasury bills... annuities... life insurance... self-sustaining businesses... franchises... Network Marketing partnerships... trusts... inheritances... and collectibles.

Each of these can be used to create **Recurring income**. By nature, I'm a conservative guy, so I'll skip some of the higher-risk investments, such as collectibles (art, antiques, rare jewelry, stamps, etc.) to concentrate on the investments that have worked for me—real estate, index funds and mutual funds, and CDs.

ABCD of Long-Term Investing

Just as the basics of reading and writing start with learning and practicing your ABCs, the basics of investing start with practicing **ABCD**.

A stands for **Automatic savings**
B stands for **Buy and hold**
C stands for **Conservative**
D stands for **Diversify**
Let's take a moment to discuss how each of these letters contributes to making you rich.

'A' Stands for Automatic Savings

We talked earlier about everyone having two jobs—**real work**, your day job where your *employer pays you*; and **R.E.A.L. work**, your evening and weekend job where *you pay yourself*.

No one would think of working a *real job* for free, would they? That would be insane! Employers wouldn't be in business for long if they refused to pay their workers. Same goes for your **R.E.A.L. job**—you can't expect to perform your **R.E.A.L. job** for free, can you? *You're not going to get R.E.A.L. and get rich unless you pay yourself first.*

> No one would think of working a real job for free, would they? You're not going to get R.E.A.L. and get rich unless you pay yourself first.

The simplest and least painful way to pay yourself for your **R.E.A.L. job** is **automatic withdrawal**. To pay yourself for doing **R.E.A.L. work**, ask your employer to withdraw a regular amount each paycheck to be deposited in a company 401(k), a personal IRA, or both.

How much should you pay yourself? That depends on how rich you want to become. Most financial advisers recommend saving 10% of your gross income (but, being the conservative guy I am, I recommend saving AT LEAST 20%). If you're an average couple earning around $50,000 a year, saving 10% of your gross means setting aside a minimum of $400 a month, which, invested in an interest-bearing account, will add up to $5,000 a year until your retirement.

Our benchmark for getting rich, you'll recall, is $1 million, not including the equity in your home, and investing $400 a month in the stock market for 40 years will net you well over $1 million. (As you will learn in the coming chapter on **Appreciation**, you can become a millionaire on just $10 a day!)

'B' Stands for Buy and Hold

Warren Buffett, the world's second-richest man and arguably the greatest investor in history, is the poster child of the **buy and hold** philosophy. Buffett's philosophy is to buy undervalued companies with great business fundamentals, such as Dairy Queen, and hold onto them for decades.

> Buy and hold won't get you rich overnight, but it will get you rich over time.

Buy and hold won't get you rich overnight, but it will get you rich over time. If you had invested $10,000 in Berkshire Hathaway in 1965, the year Buffett took control, by 2005, 40 years later, your $10,000 would be worth $30 million.

Okay, I know, some of you are thinking that 40 years is a long time. Sure is. But $30 million is a lot of money, and because life expectancy in the U.S. today is nearing 80 years, you'll likely work 40-50 years before retirement. Wouldn't you rather live a worry-free, luxurious lifestyle during your retirement years? You can when you buy the right real estate and stocks. (By the way, if you're looking to get rich buying and holding stock in Berkshire Hathaway, you're likely too late. Last time I looked, the stock was priced at *$106,000 a share!*)

In the next chapter, we'll talk more about how buying and holding can make you a millionaire.

'C' Stands for Conservative

Unlike many amateur investors, Buffett doesn't invest in hot stock tips or "can't miss" Internet stocks, hoping to make a bundle by buying the next Microsoft or Google when it's selling for $1 a share and selling it a few months later when the share price hits $100.

Buffett owns dozens of companies, but not a single share of tech stocks. Instead, he sticks with boring, old-economy companies that keep pumping out profits year after year—Benjamin Moore paints... Mohawk carpets... GEICO insurance... See's candy... Borsheim's jewelry. His favorite companies are so conservative. So boring. So predictable. And so profitable.

Buffett has been known to spend billions to buy a single company, but that doesn't make him a gambler. Conservative by nature, Buffett makes huge moves in the marketplace only after intensive research. He recognizes there are no guarantees in life, but he

> Diversifying allows you to take some of the highs and lows out of the roller coaster ride.

also understands you can stack the odds in your favor by doing your homework and investing for the long haul.

Although his net worth is approaching $50 billion, Buffett is still **Conservative** with a capital C. He has lived in the same house he first purchased in 1958 for $31,000. Today, houses in his neighborhood can still be purchased for under $200,000. He buys his cars for cash and keeps them a minimum of five years. The vanity license plate on his American-made car is a testimony to his conservative philosophy. The rear plate reads THRIFTY.

'D' Stands for Diversify

No doubt you've heard the expression "Don't put all your eggs in one basket." That's a folksy way of saying **diversify**.

To **get R.E.A.L. and get rich**, you have to invest your money or your time—and sometimes both. And any time you invest, whether it's in the market or real estate or a new business venture, there's always a risk you could end up losing money.

That's why **diversifying** is essential to wealth creation. The majority of my assets were in real estate, but even within that sector, I always maintained diversity. I still own a few rental houses, but in the past I've owned duplexes and apartment buildings... strip malls... commercial property... and raw land.

Same goes for my market holdings. Within my IRAs, 401(k)s, and individual accounts, I own a variety of mutual funds and index funds, as well as bonds and CDs. I've been an investor long enough to know that markets travel like roller coasters, with gradual climbs upward, followed by stomach-churning lows, only to level off and start climbing again.

Diversifying allows you to take some of the highs and lows out of the roller coaster ride. **Diversification** makes the ride less thrilling, but it will guarantee that you arrive at your destination of financial freedom, rather than crashing at the bottom of a long dive.

Diversify Your Income Streams

Just as it's important to diversify your investments, it's also important to **diversify your income stream**. Fifty years ago there was such as thing as "job security." Not anymore. The world of business is so competitive and fast-changing today that employers can't guarantee their employees lifetime positions.

New day, new rules.

And one of the new rules for employees is to be loyal to your employer, but *be even more loyal to yourself.* Meaning you have to establish **multiple streams of income** to protect yourself in the event you're downsized or your job is outsourced.

> You have to establish multiple streams of income to protect yourself.

Earlier we talked about **real work**—the work you get paid for at your day job; vs. **R.E.A.L. work**—the work you get paid for during your evenings and weekends. One way to create an income stream in a short period of time is to use your free time to build a **Network Marketing business**. Unlike traditional businesses, Network Marketing can generate a stream of income that will enable you to build recurring income on a *short-term 4-to-5-year plan*, instead of the *long-term 40-to-50-year plan* that most retirement portfolios are based upon.

But before we learn how Networking can help you **Get R.E.A.L. and get rich**, let's turn to the next chapter to see how the second letter in the **R.E.A.L.** acronym—the letter **E** for **Equity**—plays a vital role in your goal of financial freedom.

Chapter 4

Equity: The Doorway to the American Dream

The instinct of ownership is fundamental to man's nature.

—William James
pioneering American psychologist

I was only seven when Castro confiscated our home in Cuba, but that humiliating incident is burned into my memory, which is why today, four decades later, I'm obsessed with owning real estate.

You see, property rights—that is, the freedom of individual citizens to own real estate—goes hand in hand with democracy and the free enterprise system. When you own property—whether it's your own home, rental property, or commercial real estate—you literally own a piece of a nation.

That's why the first act of communist leaders is to outlaw private property and turn it over to the state. Ruthless communist dictators such as Castro, Mao, Lenin, and the like understood that whoever owns the property owns the power. And in communist countries, a few top-level leaders control all the property and have all the power, while the masses of people have neither.

Advantages of Owning vs. Renting

Unlike Cuba, the U.S. government encourages citizens to own real estate. When you own real estate, especially a home, you become a stockholder in U.S.A. Corp. As a homeowner, you're vested... you own a piece of the rock, so to speak. You enjoy pride of ownership. And you're king and queen of your own domain, no matter how humble it may be.

But the biggest advantage of home ownership comes down to dollars and cents—owning a home is a great business move. Not only does the government allow you to deduct your property taxes and interest payments (in 2005, 35 million taxpayers deducted an average of $9,650 of mortgage interest), but, as a homeowner, you *make money* by **building equity** each month—unlike renters, who must *spend money* while building their landlord's equity.

Equity.

It's the main reason nearly 70% of North Americans own their own homes. Home equity is easy to calculate. Just subtract the balance you owe on your mortgage (let's say $150,000) from the market value of your home (let's say $250,000). The balance is your equity ($100,000), which is pretty close to the average for U.S. homeowners.

Home equity is a Savings account, not a Spending account.

For the vast majority of Americans, **equity in their homes** is by far their biggest asset. In the previous chapter, we talked about the "**ABCD of long-term investing**," with the **A** standing for **Automatic savings**. Well, home ownership is the **ultimate Automatic savings plan**. You make a mortgage payment each month, and the amount that is applied to your principle plus your home's appreciation (more about that in the next chapter) is "automatically deposited" into your equity.

Home Equity: a Savings Account, Not a Debit Card

Now, notice I said that home equity is a **Savings account**, not a **Spending account**. Easy access to low-interest home equity loans has enabled millions of people to tap into their home equity.

In 1968, the average home contained $65,000 in equity. Back then, most homeowners didn't tap into their equity, choosing instead to retire their mortgages and leave their homes to their children. Flashing forward to 2006, the average home contains $110,000 in equity, nearly double the amount of 40 years ago. But unlike our parents, today's generation is cashing out their home equity—*$640 billion in 2006 alone.*

So, what are Americans spending their equity on? Not surprisingly, research shows that the higher the homeowner's income bracket, the more likely they will use their **home equity loans** to buy assets that will increase their net worth, such as real estate. The lower the income, the more likely the homeowner will use their equity to spend on vacations, travel, and depreciable items, such as big-screen TVs, that will decrease their net worth.

> The higher the homeowner's income bracket, the more likely they will use their home equity loans to buy assets that will increase their net worth.

Goes to show you that people who **get R.E.A.L.**, are the ones who **get rich** and **stay rich**. Rich people protect their equity or use it to create even more wealth, whereas all too many middle class people treat their equity like a debit card and squander it on TVs and trips… and just get deeper in debt.

Four Types of Equity

Although it's the most common, **home equity** is only one of four major types of equity. The other three equities are **real estate investments… stocks and bonds… and business ownership.** Let's take a moment to examine each of these equities in more detail to see how each is essential for **getting R.E.A.L. and getting rich**.

Equity in Your Home

As I already pointed out, **home equity** is the average family's biggest asset—by far. It's good that 70% of Americans own their own homes. *However, it's NOT good that most people have few assets outside their homes.* To be truly rich, my rule of thumb is to

> All too many middle class people treat their equity like a debit card and squander it on TVs and trips.

accumulate at least $1 million of assets other than your home. By all means, make home ownership your top priority (97% of millionaires own their homes). But when calculating your net worth, just don't include your home in the equation.

Why would I say such a thing? Because I figure you have to live somewhere, so if you sell your home, you'll have to buy another. Or if you sell your home and rent a place, you'll be spending your assets instead of growing them. Or if you get a reverse mortgage and use the proceeds to live on, you'll be selling your home equity for wholesale while whittling away your assets. So, my advice is to pretend the equity in your home doesn't exist and concentrate on increasing equity in the other key areas.

I'll offer three tips to managing your home equity so that you **get rich... and stay rich**.

Tip 1: Avoid the temptation to buy more home than you can really afford. A lot of homebuyers become "house poor" because they calculate the biggest monthly mortgage they can afford and then seek homes in that price range. Lenders have lowered their lending standards so that, today, applicants can qualify for monthly house payments equivalent to almost 50% of their monthly gross income. The monthly gross income for the average household is $4,200, which means they may qualify for a monthly mortgage payment of $2,000 (to include **P.I.T.I.**, that is, **Principle, Interest, Taxes, and Insurance**). A good rule of thumb for calculating how much a couple will need to cover their monthly mortgage payment is "$10 of mortgage payment for each $1,000 of the total mortgage amount." For example, with little or no money down, a couple with $2,000 a month to spend on their mortgage can afford a $200,000 home ($10 x 200 thousands = $2,000 per month) based on a 30-year mortgage at a fixed rate of 7%. **Warning:** If the couple stretches their mortgage payment to the max, they may end up with their dream home, but, after deducting income and Social Security taxes from their gross monthly income, they'll only end up with $1,000 a month to live on. Which means they'll be tempted to use their credit cards to support their lifestyle, sucking them up into an endless cycle of credit card debt.

Tip 2: *Buy the worst house in the best neighborhood.* I've followed this advice for years, and I've always come out ahead when it was time to move up to a nicer home. Great neighborhoods will always be in high demand, and even the best neighborhoods have houses that have fallen into disrepair. Dilapidated houses in great areas of town aren't eyesores—*they're opportunities!* Houses in need of work can be bought at a 20% to 40% discount, and many times all they need is a few thousand dollars of cosmetics, like trees and bushes trimmed, a fresh paint job, new carpet, and colorful landscaping. Buy a run-down house for $200,000 in a neighborhood of $250,000 houses, invest evenings and weekends making it sparkle like new, and your home equity can surge $40,000 to $50,000 in a few months.

> Dilapidated houses in great areas of town aren't eyesores— they're opportunities!

Tip 3: *Join the gentrification movement.* Right now, dozens of distressed neighborhoods all across the country are being renovated and revitalized as more and more people are moving from the suburbs back to the inner city. Once-dilapidated downtown areas of Pittsburgh... Chicago... Los Angeles... Miami... and Tampa, to name a few, are booming, drawing thousands of new residents and scores of new businesses. Revitalized neighborhoods offer lots of opportunity to get **big boosts in equity**, especially for the pioneers who get in early. The upside of getting in early is that you get the pick of the best properties at rock-bottom prices. The downside to pioneering is twofold: One, it may take years for a distressed area to turn around, and getting in early may mean exposing yourself to high crime rates and unsavory neighbors; and two, if the area fails to catch on as you anticipate, you may end up with an over-improved property in a bad part of town that is destined to remain that way. For the record, I've made substantial profits by buying and renovating in gentrified areas. The bigger the risk, the bigger the reward. Conversely, the bigger the risk, the bigger the loss if your vision is clouded or others don't follow suit.

Equity in Real Estate Investments

Real estate is where the lion's share of my net worth came from, so I'm all in favor of your owning investment properties.

Having said that, just because you own an income property doesn't automatically guarantee it's a great investment. To make money in real estate, you have to buy the **right property...** at the **right time...** in the **right location...** for the **right price**. Do all those things and real estate can make you rich. But do three of those things and miss out on just one—like buying at the *wrong time*—and what you thought was a great investment can drain your assets one mortgage payment at a time.

There's been a big run up in the value of single-family homes since the dot-com bust in 2000. Part of the increase in home prices came from pent-up demand. But in many areas of the country, prices jumped 50% to 100% or more as the result of speculators looking to make a quick buck. The difference between a real estate speculator and investor is simple.

> Speculators are banking on fast appreciation. Investors are looking for their properties to throw off a positive cash flow while appreciating slowly over time.

Speculators are banking on fast appreciation. In Florida, where I live, speculators would buy condos before the developer broke ground, hoping to make $20,000 to $200,000 by selling their units as the buildings neared completion. The speculators who bought and sold early in the boom cycle made a bundle. The speculators who bought at the top of the cycle stand to lose a bundle.

Investors, on the other hand, are looking for their properties to throw off a positive cash flow while appreciating slowly over time. Successful real estate investors have to do their homework because for the "numbers to work," the monthly rent has to exceed the monthly overhead. Successful investors are good at evaluating properties, and they understand market trends. When the numbers don't work, they walk away, knowing there is always another deal that makes sense.

The best advice I ever received about buying investment property came from a former CPA who's a very conservative real estate investor. For every property he buys, he evaluates hundreds of others and makes dozens of low-ball offers that are turned down. His advice has saved me from making big mistakes and has made me millions. Here it is: *"In real estate, you make money when you buy, not when you sell."* In other words, buying real estate is like participating in an auction. Successful buyers set a ceiling on what the item is worth (and that ceiling is often 20% to 50% below appraised value). If they can get it for that price or less, they buy. If not, they walk away.

> Over the long term, stocks outperform bonds.

The investors who get caught up in a bidding war or "fall in love with a property" and pay more for the property than the numbers support are the ones who will sell for a loss a few years later. And guess who will buy their property at a fire sale or foreclosure? The same savvy investors who passed on the property when the price was too high.

As I write this, I'm not buying any more property in Florida and California until the prices come down and the numbers start to make sense again. Speculators in both states have driven real estate prices way beyond their intrinsic value, and insurance and property taxes have gone through the roof, so I'm sitting on the sidelines until the numbers make sense again. So should you.

Remember: *In real estate, you make money when you buy, not when you sell.* Buy right and you can get rich. Buy wrong and you can get burned.

Equity in Stocks and Bonds

Stocks are also known as **equities** because when you buy a share of stock, you literally own equity in the company. When you buy a **bond**, on the other hand, you're lending money to a company, city, or country. Over the long term, **stocks outperform bonds** and, according to some researchers, are even less risky than bonds, so I'll focus on how to buy stocks to get **R.E.A.L. and get rich**.

The two biggest excuses for not investing in the stock market are one, stocks can go down, or worse, stock markets can crash: and two, "I don't have the extra money."

Let's deal with objection two first—**I don't have the extra money.** My response is, "Yes, you do—you're just choosing to spend it on something else." Cell phones didn't exist 25 years ago, yet millions of people are finding an extra $100 a month for cell phone service. TV was free when there were only three networks, but the average household is finding an extra $75 a month for cable TV.

> If you invest at the top of a bull market before it dives, on average you'll make up your loss in two years.

I'm not suggesting you give up cell phones and cable TV—I'm just suggesting you "find" the money for the things you value. I value security and a rich retirement, which is why I found the money to invest in **stocks** and **real estate**. So, if you honestly want to **get R.E.A.L. and get rich**, you'll find the money. If you don't really want to get rich, you won't find the money. Simple as that.

As for the first objection—**stocks go down and markets crash**—you're right. In 1929, the market crashed and dragged the country into the Great Depression. More recently, in 1987, the Dow Jones Industrial Average fell a gut-wrenching 23% in just one day! Hey, if you're looking for excuses NOT to invest in the stock market, I just gave you two classic ones. Yes, markets go down, and sometimes they plunge. But over time, markets go up far more often and at far faster rates than they go down.

The key is not to panic when the market takes a dive. Markets that go down are called **bear markets**. Markets that go up are called **bull markets**. Amateur investors often panic when the market goes down, selling their stocks for a loss. The first rule of **Stock Investing 101** is to **buy low, sell high**. People who jump in when the market is going up and sell when it's going down are doing the opposite—they're buying high and selling low. Smart investors don't panic when the market drops. They wait until the bottom and buy more stocks because prices are lower.

The key is to buy great stocks for the long term and then hold on through the **bear markets**. The data shows that since WWII, investors who stayed invested during a bear market have been able to recoup 120% of what they lost by the second year of the new **bull market**. So, if you're in for the long haul, even if you invest at the top of a **bull market** just before it dives, on average you'll make up your loss PLUS another 20% in the next two years.

Stocks vs. Other Assets

Below is a graph showing how stocks have outperformed other asset classes over the last two centuries, proving that stocks should be one of the cornerstones for anyone who wants to **get R.E.A.L. and get rich**.

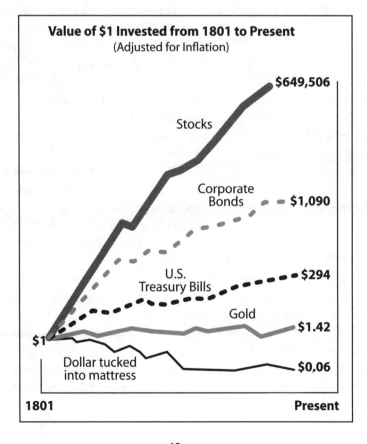

Value of $1 Invested from 1801 to Present
(Adjusted for Inflation)

$649,506

Stocks

Corporate Bonds — $1,090

U.S. Treasury Bills — $294

Gold

$1.42

$1

Dollar tucked into mattress — $0.06

1801   Present

I repeat: The secret to making money in the stock market is to buy great stocks (or better yet, several index funds) and hold them for years, over the good times and the bad. As market expert Jeremy Siegel, author of *The Future for Investors*, says:

"Over short periods, stocks are undoubtedly riskier than bonds. But as the holding period increases to between 15 and 20 years, the riskiness of stocks falls below that of fixed-income assets. And over 30-year periods, stock risk falls to less than three-quarters the risk of bonds or T-bills."

Warren Buffett echoes the same philosophy with this one-word reply to a reporter who asked history's greatest stock-picker when was the best time to sell stocks:

"Never," said Buffett.

So, if stocks are such a great investment, who owns them?

The short answer to the question "Who owns stocks?" is "Rich people do." Owning stocks is how rich people get rich... and stay rich. The facts bear this out. The wealthiest 20% of households own more than 90% of all stock value, with the wealthiest 1% owning an average of $3.3 million in stocks. What about the less-than-rich?—how much stock do they own? Not enough. Sadly, less than 50% of Americans own any stock at all, and only 33% of households own more than $5,000 in stocks.

> The wealthiest 20% of households own more than 90% of all stock value, with the wealthiest 1% owning an average of $3.3 million in stocks. Sadly, less than 50% of Americans own any stock at all.

Okay, let's pause to ponder this question. *If you want to get rich, what's one thing you can do that rich people are doing?* That's right— **own stocks!** But if you want to remain poor or middle class, then do what 50% of Americans are doing—instead of buying **equities that increase in value** (like Apple Computer), buy consumer **products that decrease in value** (like i-Pods) sold by public companies so that the stockholders in those companies can get richer while you get poorer.

Here are four tips for getting rich with stocks. These tips are working for millions of **Millionaires Next Door**—and they can work for you.

Tip 1: Max out tax-deferred accounts. The old cliché that you can't escape death or taxes is true—but you *CAN* **delay taxes for decades** through tax-deferred investment vehicles, such as **IRAs** and **401(k)s**. You can invest up to $4,000 a year in a **tax-deferred IRA** ($5,000 if you're 50 or older) or in a **tax-free Roth IRA** (Roth IRAs are taxed upfront at your current federal tax rate but can be withdrawn TAX FREE at maturity). If your employer offers a **401(k)**, they're begging you to accept FREE MONEY because they match a percentage of your salary (usually from 3% to 5%) and hand it to you to **compound** (more about compounding in the next chapter) inside a tax-deferred vehicle. You wouldn't turn down a tax-free raise, would you? You wouldn't walk past a $100 bill on the street and not pick it up, would you? Then why turn down an **employer-sponsored 401(k)**? Get enrolled—today!

> You wouldn't turn down a tax-free raise, would you? You wouldn't walk past a $100 bill on the street and not pick it up, would you? Then why turn down an employer-sponsored 401(k)?

Tip 2: Buy index funds and exchange-traded funds (ETFs). There are 9,000 publicly traded companies in the U.S. alone, so how do you separate the winners from the losers?

Here's my advice—**don't even try**.

Mutual fund managers are mathematical whizzes with Ivy League degrees. They employ only the smartest of the smart economists and research analysts from around the world... they monitor sophisticated computer models to analyze the market 24/7... and they study the market 16 hours a day. Yet, despite all of those advantages, in a given year, **only 20% of the mutual fund managers outperform the S&P**

500, the performance benchmark composed of 500 of the biggest publicly traded companies in the U.S.

So I ask you—if the **S&P 500** beats the brainiest guys and gals on Wall Street four out of every five years, why not just buy all of the stocks in the **S&P 500** and forget about it? Well, that's exactly what I recommend you do—buy **index funds**, a collection of stocks in a given stock market, instead of trying to pick individual stocks or top-performing **mutual funds**. Unlike mutual funds that can charge 5% a year for management fees, index funds charge a fraction of 1%, saving you possibly tens of thousands over the lifetime of your investments.

> In a given year, only 20% of the mutual fund managers outperform the S&P 500.

According to Jack Bogle, founder of the **Vanguard Group** and the father of the **index funds**, there are 12 U.S. and international stock market index funds available to investors. The **S&P 500** is the mother of all market measures for U.S. stocks, dating back to 1896. India's version is the **Bombay Stock Exchange 100**, which has returned an average of 15.30% for the 10-year period ending in 2006.

Exchange-traded funds (ETFs) are index funds focused on sectors and themes, such as large companies… mid-size companies… utilities… transportation… healthcare—the list goes on. As I write this, there are 340 **ETFs** available, offering a wide range of investment choices. **Vanguard** offers more than 30 **ETFs**, many of which have consistently outperformed the vast majority of mutual funds. For more information about index funds and **ETFs** and to review their performance histories, go to any of these sites:

Vanguard.com
Fidelity.com
Morningstar.com

Tip 3: Be conservative and diversify. In 1945, at the close of WWII, the U.S. was at the height of its economic power, with one out of every two dollars in the world flowing into U.S. companies. The

U.S. was the leading manufacturer and consumer in the world, and U.S. companies dominated the stock market.

Those days are over.

Today, the U.S. accounts for just 22% of the world economy, and it's dropping like a stone. As respected economist and author Jeremy Siegel says, "The U.S. over time will become a narrower and narrower slice of the world market." That's bad news if you've got a job in manufacturing, but good news if you're an investor.

Because of **index funds** and **ETFs** and the proliferation of **online brokerages**, it's easy for investors to buy stocks in regions of the world that are booming, like Brazil, Russia, India, and China (**BRIC**). Yes, the U.S. is still a great place to invest, but today, more than ever, you must diversify your holdings not only across sectors but also around the world.

An easy way to diversify is to invest in a concept dubbed **lifecycle funds**, which are designed as the ultimate buy-and-forget investment. The concept is simple and works well for people who have no interest in following the market, which is most of us. To get started, you choose a lifecycle fund based on your retirement date. If you have 40 years before retirement, for example, the fund will be weighted toward stocks—something like 90% stocks and 10% bonds. As you get closer

> Today, more than ever, you must diversify your holdings not only across sectors but also around the world.

to retirement, the fund is automatically rebalanced to reduce risk, moving away from stocks, which are riskier than bonds in the short term, and into fixed-income investments, such as bonds, CDs, and money market funds.

Tip 4: Learn to earn. The advice from *Why We Want You to Be Rich* by Donald Trump and Robert Kiyosaki that I quoted early in this book bears repeating: "You cannot solve money problems with money. **You can only solve money problems with education**." To get rich, first, you must become a student of wealth-building principles. Second, you must act on the things you've learned.

I know a lot of poor and middle-class people who tell me they want to get rich, but who keep doing the same things—spending instead of saving and investing—and then they whine that they're fearful about their financial future, but they don't know what to do about it. Yet, when I ask them if they have taken any investment classes or read any books on investing, they fidget and say something like, "I just can't get interested in that stuff" or "I'm not very good with finances."

These people remind me of a *Non Sequitur* cartoon I saw in the local newspaper. A man in a winter coat and hat is sitting on a box and holding a fishing pole over what appears to be a hole in the ice on a frozen lake. On the horizon, just a few feet away, is a golfer holding a putter. Between the two men is a golf ball. It's obvious the fisherman is on a golf course, not a frozen lake. The caption reads: *"Larry begins to form a hypothesis on why the fish aren't biting."*

Just as Larry can't catch fish on a golf course, you can't get rich by spending your assets. Like Larry, if your current strategy is doomed to failure, you have to form a new hypothesis that will help you accomplish your goal. It's never too late to learn about investing, and with the advent of the Internet, there's a wealth of easily accessible, easy-to-understand, free information about investing.

> Rich people not only own their own homes, they're also likely to own a business.

The more you learn, the more you earn. Here are two great sites that will educate you on a wide variety of financial issues:

Fool.com—The odd name comes from the expression "motley fool," which refers to a court jester who, through humor and wit, could tell the king the truth while the rest of the court had to tell lies to curry favor.

Binarydollar.com—The word "binary" refers to the binary code used to store data in personal computers. Tons of information and new stuff each day make regular visits to this site worthwhile.

There are, of course, hundreds of other worthwhile sites offering education and advice about your finances. Google "investing" or "stocks" or "personal finances," and you'll gain access to more useful information than you could read in your lifetime.

Equity in Businesses

Rich people not only own their own homes (97% of millionaires are homeowners) and own stocks, they're also likely to own a business. As the authors of *The Millionaire Next Door* point out, "Self-employed people make up less than 20% of the people in America but account for *two-thirds of the millionaires*."

The lesson is clear—**if you want to get rich, you need to own your own business**. Americans may not be saving and investing, but to their credit, they ARE starting businesses in record numbers. According to the Small Business Administration, 672,000 new companies with employees were created in 2006, along with more than 2 million sole proprietorships.

Small business is, and always has been, the backbone of the American economy, employing 70% of workers. Sole proprietorships still dominate small business in North America, with 20 million Americans working solo, accounting for 75% of all small businesses.

North Americans are not alone in wanting to own their own businesses—more than 80% of all businesses around the world are family-owned—but we ARE still the most entrepreneurial country in the world.

Why are North Americans so prone to going it alone?

It's partly due to a culture that admires and honors independence.

It's partly due to a political system that makes it cheap and easy to start up your own enterprise.

It's partly due to wage stagnation, as wage increases have averaged 1% a year since 2002, while home prices have almost doubled in the same period.

It's partly due to lack of job security in corporate America (between 70,000 and 80,000 workers are being laid off EVERY MONTH in the U.S. even though the economy is booming).

It's partly due to our genes, as North America was populated primarily by immigrants who had the will, optimism, and daring to leave their home countries and take a leap into the unknown, passing those traits down to us, their descendants.

But it's mostly due to every human's inborn desire to own their own lives by making their own decisions... running their own show... being their own boss... calling their own shots.

Don't Know Where to Start

Yep, entrepreneurship is alive and well in America these days. A recent survey by yahoo.com indicated that 66% of respondents wanted to start a company someday, with almost 40% hoping to do so within the next five years.

So, what's holding back all of these would-be entrepreneurs? Not surprisingly, the biggest thing holding people back from starting their own business is "they don't know where to begin," according to a survey by Capital One and Consumer Action. In other words, millions of Americans have the *want to* to start their own business, but they lack the *how to*.

> 66% of Americans wanted to start a company someday, with almost 40% hoping to do so within the next five years.

Little wonder, then, that **franchising** is exploding across North America and the rest of the world. **Franchising**, with its copycat business model, enables aspiring business owners to duplicate an existing, successful business model, thereby reducing the risk and increasing the chances for success.

But with initial franchising costs averaging $250,000, excluding real estate, only people with deep pockets and a lot of business experience are viable candidates to open a new franchise—and even then, there are no guarantees of success.

Thanks, but no thanks.

Average people are priced out of the franchising business model. But virtually anyone can afford—and can succeed in—a **franchise-like business model called Network Marketing**, which has all of the copycat features of franchising at a fraction of the cost.

Network Marketing enables people to tap into their **inner entrepreneur** and own their own business even though they "don't know where to begin." **Network Marketing** will not only show you where to begin, but will give you a proven, connect-the-dots business plan that tens of thousands of people have followed to get **R.E.A.L. and get rich**.

In Chapter 7, we'll discuss in depth the benefits of owning your own business before explaining why **Network Marketing** is the ideal business for the 21st century.

Average people are priced out of the franchising business model. But virtually anyone can afford—and can succeed in—a franchise-like business model called Network Marketing.

But first, let's turn to the next chapter to see how the third letter in the get **R.E.A.L. formula—A for Appreciation**—has helped both big and small investors to multiply their money many times over. Turn the page to discover how they do it.

Chapter 5

Appreciation: How to Turn a Molehill of Savings into a Mountain of Money

Nowadays, people can be divided into three classes: The Haves, the Have-Nots, and the Have–Not– Paid–for–What–They–Haves.

—Earl Wilson
American newspaper columnist

How many times have you driven by a luxury apartment complex and seen a late-model BMW or Mercedes parked out front? Happens to me almost daily.

Many people might envy such a sight. Not me. I have the opposite feeling—I get depressed. Why? Because when I see expensive cars parked outside expensive apartments, all I see is money being flushed down the drain.

Slurp... $2,000 (or more) *a month* for rent... down the drain
Slurp... $500 (or more) *a month* for car lease... down the drain
Slurp... $30,000 *A YEAR*... down the drain

Renting an apartment and leasing a car are classic examples of **depreciation**. When something depreciates, it goes down in value (or, in the case of renting and leasing, the money disappears, never to be seen again). Buying depreciable products and services is like visiting an ATM, withdrawing $500, and then tossing the money out the car window as you drive away.

No one in their right mind would do that, would they?

Yet that's exactly what people do when they spend their hard-earned money on **depreciable assets**, like expensive cars; or on **liabilities**, like renting luxury condos. Not only are they tossing away the immediate use of their money, but they're also tossing away the opportunity for that money to grow through **appreciation**.

To illustrate the power of **appreciation**, let's take a look at what would happen if a newly married couple in their mid-20s who are currently spending $30,000 a year renting a fancy apartment and leasing a new car were to buy a starter home with a monthly mortgage of $1,000 (instead of throwing away $2,000 on rent) and a used car with a monthly loan payment of $250 (instead of throwing away $500 on a lease) and then invested the $15,000 difference in appreciable assets, like a portfolio of **index funds** averaging 10% a year. By the time they were ready for retirement at age 65, their *$15,000 investment would have grown to more than $600,000!*

> "Rich people acquire assets. The poor and middle class acquire liabilities but think they are assets."

Ask yourself this question: When you retire, would you prefer to have nothing of value to show for your early years of marriage except dim memories of fancy cars and luxury apartments? Or would you prefer to have $600,000 in your retirement account PLUS free title to your own home?

That's a no-brainer if there ever was one!

Appreciation Grows, Depreciation Goes

Rich people understand the **power of appreciation** and set aside a portion of their income to *invest in things that continue to grow in* *value*, such as homes, businesses, stocks, real estate, education and training, and so on. The poor and middle class, on the other hand, set aside little or none of their income, but instead, they *buy things that depreciate in value*, like new cars, new furniture, and new flat-screen TVs (even though the old TVs work just fine).

As Robert Kiyosaki observes in *Rich Dad, Poor Dad*, "Rich people acquire assets. The poor and middle class acquire liabilities but think they are assets." Kiyosaki calls this "Rule One" and says if you want to get rich, Rule One is the only rule you need to know.

I have my own saying: "**Appreciation grows; depreciation goes**."

When your **money goes**, it's gone forever. Poof! Vanished! But when your **money grows**, it creates income not only during your lifetime, but, if you place your assets in a trust, your money can continue to grow long after your time on this earth is over.

I have to laugh when I hear people justify the purchase of a luxury car by saying, "It will hold its value." Truth is, no car holds its value unless it's an antique in mint condition or a rare classic. According to Kelly Bluebook, a leading provider of new- and used-vehicle information, the average vehicle retains about 35% of its original value after five years. Which means a Mercedes E350 that cost $50,000 new is worth $17,500 five years later, a loss of $32,500.

> Compounding is like the snowball effect—it gets bigger and bigger as it rolls along.

Look, if you're determined to buy a Mercedes E350, doesn't it make sense to buy a five-year-old model for less than $20,000 and then invest the $30,000 difference in an **appreciable asset**? That way, you can enjoy the status and luxury of a Mercedes while building wealth for the future.

The Magic of Compounding

To understand how **appreciation** can make you wealthy, you first need to learn about a simple mathematical principle called "**compounding**." It's so powerful that Einstein called it the "eighth wonder of the world."

Compounding is like the snowball effect—it gets bigger and bigger as it rolls along. Let's say your nest egg is $1,000, and you invest it in an **index fund** that returns 10% interest per year. At the end of 12 months, you'd have a total of $1,100. The next year you'd earn 10% interest on $1,100, which adds up to $1,210 at the end of year two. Leave the money in to compound at 10%, and in a little more than seven years your $1,000 investment would have doubled to $2,000. After 14 years, that $2,000 would double again to $4,000.

The **doubling effect** is the key to the **magic of compounding**. The longer you leave the money in, the more time it has to double over and over. Allow that $1,000 to compound at 10% during your entire 50-year working career, and by the time you retire, that $1,000 nest egg will have grown to more than $60,000! And that's from just a $1,000 investment. If that $1,000 investment were $10,000, it would have grown to $600,000—that's serious money in anybody's book.

> The doubling effect is the key to the magic of compounding. Allow $1,000 to compound at 10% during your entire 50-year working career, and by the time you retire, that $1,000 nest egg will have grown to more than $60,000!

The Earlier You Start, the Richer You Get

The most amazing thing about *compounding* is that the *amount of time invested* is even more important than the *amount of money invested*, so the sooner you start saving and investing—even if it's a small amount—the bigger your payoff will be when you reach retirement age. To take full advantage of compounding, it's better to invest a small amount at a young age than a big amount later.

For example, let's say two young college graduates, Abby and Arturo, both 22 years old, have started working for the same company earning the same pay. Their pay is low, so money is tight. But Abby understands the **power of compounding,** so she doggedly invests $83.33 a month, or $1,000 a year, in a tax-deferred IRA earning 10% a year. She does this for eight years, from age 22 until age 30, when she resigns to be a stay-at-home mom. **Her total investment is only $8,000,** which she keeps in her IRA until she retires at age 65.

> It's better to invest a small amount at a young age than a big amount later.

Arturo, on the other hand, chooses not to put any money aside until age 30, when he has more disposable income. But he's wise enough to know he has to play catch-up because he neglected to invest in his 20s, so, beginning at age 30, he invests $1,000 a year earning 10% in his IRA until he retires at age 65 for **a total investment of $35,000.**

So, who do you think will have the biggest nest egg by age 65? Abby, who only invested $8,000 beginning at age 22? Or Arturo, who invested $35,000 beginning at age 30, more than three times the amount Abby invested?

Mary invested $8,000 @ 10% for 43 years	Arturo invested $35,000 @ 10% for 35 years
Total at 65 = **$388,865**	Total at 65 = **$329,039**

Amazingly, Arturo invested three times more money but never caught up. Why? Because of the **doubling effect of compounding.** The longer your money is left to grow tax-deferred, the bigger your payoff will be at the end of the retirement rainbow.

Become a Millionaire for $10 a Day

Let me ask you a question. If a stranger came up to you on a Monday and said he would give you a million dollars if you could save just $10 a day for an entire week, could you come up with $70 by Sunday evening? You'd find that $10 a day, even if you were unemployed at the time, wouldn't you?

Well, becoming a millionaire is just that simple, but instead of putting away $10 a day for ONE week, you have to do it **EVERY DAY FOR EVERY WEEK OF THE YEAR, week in and week out, year in and year out, for 35 years.** (The fact you can do it one week just proves you can do it every week if you put your mind to it.)

> By investing only $10 a day at 10% interest, at the end of 35 years, you'd have $1,016,203 in your account.

By investing only $10 a day (a small, doable number that adds up to $300 a month, or $3,650 a year) at 10% interest (which is less than the U.S. stock market has averaged annually since 1926), at the end of 35 years, you'd have $1,016,203 in your account.

Congratulations—*you're a millionaire.*

How can such a small daily contribution turn into a million dollars?

Compounding.

See, the **magic of compounding** is that your money continues to **double**, even when the numbers get huge. For example, by investing $10 a day at 10%, by the end of 20 years, you would have accumulated $230,974. By year 27, that $230,974 would **double** again to $461,947. And in seven more years by year 34, the $461,947 would **double** yet again to $923,894.

Math for Dummies: Rule of 72

The key to taking full advantage of compounding is to start early because the biggest gains are on the back end. A thousand dollars doubled is nice money, but not huge money. A hundred thousand dollars doubled once… twice… three times makes you a few years away from joining the millionaire club.

There's a simple way to calculate how long it will take for your money to double. It's called the **Rule of 72**, and it works like this: To find the number of years it will take to **double your money**, divide the interest rate you get on your investment into 72. A 10% rate of interest, for example, would **double your money** in 7.2 years. The **Rule of 72** works in reverse, also. If you want your money to double in 6 years, for example, divide 6 into 72 and you discover you'd need your investment to earn 12%.

If you're invested in the stock market, there's no guarantee that your investment will return 10% during every seven-year span. Stock markets go up... they go down... and they even remain flat for long periods. But averaged out over your working career, history has shown that the market will return around 10%.

If you're great at picking winning stocks, you can do much better than 10%. Warren Buffett has averaged a return of 22% for nearly 40 years. Applying the **Rule of 72** to Buffett's rate of return shows he doubles his money every 3.27 years! No wonder the guy can afford to donate **$37 BILLION** to charity.

A Little Percentage Can Mean a Lot

Fortunately, to **get R.E.A.L. and get rich**, you don't have to pick stocks like Warren Buffett. Only 20% of the super-smart and/or super-lucky mutual fund managers beat the market indexes in any given year.

That's why I advise you to stick with **index funds** instead of investing in mutual funds. Besides, mutual fund managers charge fees for their services, even in bad years. If you have $50,000 invested in a fund that averages 10% returns but the manager charges 2% a year, your return is only 8% instead of 10%.

The average mutual fund management fee is near 1.5%, compared to the average fee for index funds, which is as low as 0.2%, a difference of 1.3%. Now, you may be thinking that 1% is small potatoes. But small percentages add up to huge dollars when it comes to **compounding**. The chart on the next page tells the tale:

What 1% a Year Can Cost You Based on an Average Annual Return of 6%	
Investment A	**Investment B**
(2% annual fee)	(1% annual fee)
2006: Invest $50,000	2006: Invest 50,000
2026: Value of **$107,055**	2026: Value of **$131,157**

In this example, that measly 1% extra over a 20-year period ends up costing you more than **$24,000 in lost revenue**. Ouch!

Investing in Single-Family Homes vs. Stocks

As I said earlier, I've earned most of my money in real estate. Real estate is a great investment, but like any investment, it's not foolproof. Though not as volatile as stocks, real estate, including single-family houses, have boom and bust cycles. More commonly, housing prices have big surges in appreciation and then remain flat for years.

Recently, the U.S. has had a big run-up in real estate values. In Florida, where I live, single-family homes doubled in value during a five-year span. Applying the **Rule of 72** tells me that for a home to **double** in five years it must appreciate at a rate of 14.5%.

That's great news if you bought a house five years ago and want to sell. But it's lousy news for buyers because they may be paying inflated prices for their homes, which I think is the case right now. Here's why I say that.

Historically, single-family homes have appreciated 3% a year since 1900, which means home values have doubled every 24 years. The typical well-maintained residence in a nice neighborhood in a vibrant city that cost $25,000 in 1945 would be worth between $150,000 and $250,000 today. But during the recent run-up, house prices doubled in 5 years, instead of

> Historically, single-family homes have appreciated 3% a year since 1900.

24 years. Plus, incomes have not kept up with home prices. That tells me that prices of single-family homes are going to stay the same for years or even drop in value as the market averages itself out.

What would $25,000 be worth today if it were invested in the stock market instead of a house since 1945? The numbers will amaze you! The U.S. stock market has averaged 10% a year since WWII. The **Rule of 72** tells us that $25,000 would double every 7.2 years at

> $25,000 growing at a modest 10% would end up multiplying to more than $10 million in 60 years.

10%. Divide 60 years by 7.2 and you get 8.33, the number of times the $25,000 nest egg would have doubled. So, what would $25,000 invested in **index funds** since 1945 at 10% be worth today?

Doubling	Year	Amount
	1945	$25,000
1	1952	$50,000
2	1959	$100,000
3	1963	$200,000
4	1970	$400,000
5	1978	$800,000
6	1985	$1.6 million
7	1992	$3.2 million
8	1997	$6.4 million
9	2004	**$12.8 million**

Would you have guessed that $25,000 growing at a modest 10% would end up multiplying to more than $10 million in 60 years?

Looking at the above chart makes it easy to see why Einstein called **compounding** the eighth wonder of the world.

If this information about the **power of compounding** is all new to you, that's okay. I was clueless about the **miracle of compounding** until my late 20s. But once I learned about the **doubling concept**, I quickly converted from being a flagrant spender to a steady saver. And once I got into the habit of saving and investing... once I started seeing my **assets appreciate...** then I became even more disciplined in my **saving** and more convinced that getting real about life and getting rich were not exclusive of each other... that even I, a Cuban immigrant who couldn't speak English... an under-achieving C student... a college drop-out with $67,000 of credit card debt... even with all those strikes against me, *in America, even I could Get R.E.A.L. and get rich*!

> Einstein called compounding the eighth wonder of the world.

Once I started to **believe** I could get rich, and once I started acting on that belief by doing the things rich people do, then I automatically became a millionaire. And so can you!

I Dare You to Adopt Some Discipline

Earlier we talked about the importance of paying yourself first. The first letter in the **ABCD plan** for getting rich is **A** for **automatic savings**. People tell me all the time that they don't have any extra money in their paychecks for automatic savings. Yet those same people will buy a new car every five years. If they had bought a good used car with low mileage instead a new car, they would have hundreds of dollars available each month for **automatic withdrawal**.

I contend that almost anyone in America can become rich if they're disciplined and start saving and investing early in their working careers. It's not too little money that's holding people back from getting rich. It's too little understanding of how **appreciation** works and too much desire for **depreciable consumer goods** that's holding them back.

Here's the good news. Compared to other eras... other countries... and other economies, it's *so easy* for the average person in North

America to become a millionaire—even if you start late. All it takes is the **discipline** to contribute a few thousand dollars a year into an IRA. The bad news is that only 17% of U.S. households made IRA contributions in 2006, which means 83 out of every 100 Americans are blowing their best chance for creating lasting wealth.

> Only 17% of U.S. households made IRA contributions in 2006, which means 83 out of every 100 Americans are blowing their best chance for creating lasting wealth.

Playing Catch Up

The beauty of compounding is that the big returns happen on the back end, so obviously, the more time you have on your side, the easier it is to get rich.

But what happens to people who only have 20 years before they retire... or, say, 10 years... or even less—is it too late for them to **get R.E.A.L. and get rich**?

The short answer is no, it's never too late. I have two suggestions to shore up your retirement portfolio. First, get a copy of David Bach's book *Start Late, Finish Rich*. He has a lot of practical advice that will help you get on an accelerated track to achieving financial freedom at a late age.

And second, take a second job and save and invest all of the income, or, better yet, consider creating wealth with the **Modern Method**, which is described in detail in Chapter 7. The **Modern Method** is a viable way to supplement the income from your day job. Better yet, if you have a ton of contacts and if you're a quick learner and hard worker, the **Modern Method** can quickly generate hundreds, perhaps even thousands, of dollars per month, and eventually outgrow the income from your full-time job.

Become a Millionaire on $10 a Day

As I said, becoming a millionaire is *so easy* virtually any household can do it. All it takes to become a millionaire is a few dollars a day, day in and day out, for decades.

I call this proven, long-term investment program the **Museum Method** because it's universally recognized and endorsed, classic, historic, and timeless—just like the treasures in museums.

The upside of the **Museum Method** is it's a relatively painless way to take advantage of **appreciation** without having to invest enormous amounts of money or take enormous risks. The downside is that it takes decades to see big results because the biggest benefits to **compounding** are on the back end.

Now, if you're like most people, you may be thinking you'd love to get rich, and you're willing to save and invest the money to do it, but you don't want to have to wait 40 years.

> All it takes to become a millionaire is a few dollars a day, day in and day out, for decades.

"I can't commit to the **Museum Method** because I may not be alive in 40 years" is the objection I hear most often. True, there are no guarantees in life. But, with the life expectancy in the U.S. nearing 80 today, odds are you'll be around to see retirement age. So, if you want to be SURE you'll retire rich, then you have to commit yourself to the **ABCD plan—Automatic savings... Budgeting... Conservative investing... and Diversification.**

The Modern Method: the Four-Year Plan

On the other hand, if you're like me, then you want it both ways—you want to be rich while you're young AND rich in your retirement. That's the best of both worlds, isn't it? That's the real **American Dream—get rich... live rich... retire rich.** Why should you have to settle for one when you can have it all?

Well, there is a way to **get R.E.A.L. and get rich...** in four to five years while retiring rich in 40 years—or sooner if you choose. I call this system of wealth creation the **Modern Method**, as opposed to the **Museum Method**.

The **Modern Method** relies on the same four principles of wealth creation as the **Museum Method—Recurring income...**

Equity... Appreciation... and **Leverage**. But by accessing modern-day technologies available to virtually everyone in the form of cell phones, computers, the Internet, e-commerce, affordable long-distance phone service, low-cost and convenient air travel, and hi-tech, modern-age products and services marketed and distributed via a modern-day business model, the process of wealth creation can be sped up and collapsed into months and years, instead of decades.

The Modern Method relies on the same four principles of wealth creation as the Museum Method. But by accessing modern-day technologies available to virtually everyone, the process of wealth creation can be sped up and collapsed into months and years, instead of decades.

Network Marketing: Appreciation on Steroids

The **Modern Method** I'm referring to is **Network Marketing**. And it's revolutionizing the way people live, work, shop, and create wealth. Because of the advances in technology, Network Marketing is just coming into its own, empowering average people like you and me to live above-average lifestyles by **compressing appreciation** into months and years, instead of decades.

But before we learn how **Networking** can help you get rich, let's turn to the next chapter to learn about the last principle in the **R.E.A.L.** formula, **Leverage**.

Chapter 6

Leverage: Multiplying Money, Time, and Efforts

As a small businessperson, you have no greater leverage than the truth.

—John Greenleaf Whittier
American poet

Leverage is the reason I first started investing in real estate back in the early 1980s. When I discovered I could **leverage** a $10,000 down payment to buy a $100,000 property, I was sold on real estate. Not only could I buy a property for 10% of its value, but I could also receive 100% of the benefits, including **recurring income, equity, appreciation,** and **tax benefits**—plus, 100% of the **profits** when I sold.

I was sold, all right—sold on **leverage**. Still am.

I first started taking advantage of **leverage in real estate** by investing a smaller sum of my money to gain access to a large amount of other people's money (**OPM**). As I got more experienced in business, I expanded to leveraging other people's time (**OPT**)... other people's efforts (**OPE**)... and even other people's contacts (**OPC**).

Let's take a moment to talk about **leverage** and why it's one of the four key principles that rich people have used for centuries to **get rich... and stay rich.**

Through Leverage, Small Efforts Get Big Results

Leverage comes from the Latin word *levare*, which means, "to make light." More than 2,000 years ago, Archimedes, the Greek mathematician and engineer, summed up the **power of leverage** with these words: "Give me a lever long enough and a place to stand, and I will move the world." Archimedes was talking about **mechanical leverage**, the engineering principle that early builders used to build the pyramids and that modern-day engineers are still using today to build skyscrapers.

> Leverage is powerful because small, singular efforts can generate big results. You see, without leverage, everything is limited to a ratio of 1:1.

But the type of **leverage** I'll be talking about in this chapter is **financial leverage**. **Leverage** is powerful because small, singular efforts (or small amounts of time or money) can generate big results. You see, without leverage, everything is limited to a **ratio of 1:1**.

Without **leverage**, one hour of work equals one hour of pay.

Without **leverage**, one dollar of money buys one dollar of goods and services (or $1 of real estate).

Without **leverage**, one business is limited to one location.

Without **leverage**, one seller can distribute products and services to one buyer at a time.

But **WITH LEVERAGE**, the **ratio is expanded** from 1:1... to 1:10. Or 1:100. Or 1:1,000. Or 1:10,000. Or 1:1,000,000 or more! **Leverage** expands the limits of time... space... money... contacts... communication... and, yes, even concepts.

When it comes to business, there are three basic ways to leverage time, money, and efforts: **traditional business, franchising,** and **Network Marketing**. Let's take a moment to look at each of these enterprises to see how they take advantage of leverage.

Traditional Business

Back in the early '80s, when I first started working at health clubs as an employee, I didn't understand how the owners were using the **principle of leverage** to get rich. As a young employee, all I understood was that I got a paycheck every two weeks. But later, after I became an owner myself, I quickly understood that employees were like the exercise machines scattered around the club—they were a necessary, cost-effective way the owners could **leverage their time and efforts**, thereby maximizing **profits**.

As an employee, I worked an eight- to 10-hour shift, which was the extent of my obligation to the company. In exchange for that obligation, I received a modest paycheck twice a month, and when I left work at the end of the day, I left my responsibilities to the company at the door.

But as an owner, I was "on call" 24/7 and my responsibilities expanded a thousand fold. I was no longer one guy responsible for one task. I was one guy responsible for ALL tasks. As an owner, I could work 24 hours a day and still not handle all my obligations, so I **leveraged my time and efforts** by hiring employees to deal with clients… accounting… marketing… scheduling, and so on.

After a few months, the money was rolling in, so I **leveraged my equity** by taking out bank loans and opening a second club… then a third… then a fourth… until I eventually owned and operated nine health clubs in the Los Angeles area.

Owning your own **traditional business** sounds great on paper—and it is great compared to being a low-salaried employee. But I soon learned that as you expand your business, the pressure on you expands also. When I had one health club, things were pretty simple: I had only one utility bill to pay… one storefront to open and close each day… one men's and one women's locker room to keep clean… one insurance payment to make… and one facility to deal with when an emergency came up.

With leverage, the ratio is expanded from 1:1… to 1:10. Or 1:100. Or 1:1,000. Or 1:10,000. Or 1:1,000,000 or more! Leverage expands the limits of time… space… money… contacts… communication… and, yes, even concepts.

But as I expanded, I was still one person, while the obligations multiplied exponentially. Seemed like all I was doing was putting out fires… running from one emergency to the next. I wasn't running the clubs—*the clubs were running me!* So, in 1988, after 10 years of owning my own clubs, I decided to sell. I not only made a nice profit, but by **leasing** the land at three of my clubs instead of selling everything outright, I was able to enjoy a **pipeline of monthly recurring income** that's still flowing into my pockets today, 20 years after the final sale was executed.

> The odds of succeeding in a traditional business are stacked against you these days.

I have to admit, luck was on my side when I was in the fitness business. There's a lot more competition today and operating costs have gone through the roof. I'm a big believer in **leveraging** your time and efforts by owning your own business, but I'm also a realist. I know the odds of succeeding in a **traditional business** are stacked against you these days. Fully 33% of all start-ups fail within two years, and fewer than 50% are still going after four years, according to the Small Business Administration. With those poor odds, it's little wonder **entrepreneurs** are looking for an advantage, which is why many small business owners are investing in **franchises**.

Franchising/Licensing

Companies with a duplicable business model have two ways to expand. One, they can become a **chain** by adding locations, financing each new location, and hiring and training employees to operate them. Or, two, they can significantly reduce the expenses of expansion by finding **equity partners** willing to invest money, time, and effort to open **franchises** in the company name. The **franchise partners** pay an up-front fee plus a percentage of gross monthly earnings, and, in return, the **franchisees** gain access to the business model, products, brand name, and marketing and advertising.

The **franchising concept** has been around for centuries, and some historians trace its origins back to 200 B.C. in China, when rickshaw drivers were allowed to buy and sell assigned sections in bustling cities. In the U.S., early **franchises** included General Motors dealerships in 1899, Coca-Cola bottling in 1901, and Rexall drug stores in 1902.

Today, **franchising** is a major contributor to the economies of the U.S. and Canada, accounting for 40 cents of every retail or service dollar spent in North America. According to the International Franchise Association, there are nearly **7,500 franchised businesses** with **400,000 franchisees** in 75 industries employing nearly 10 million workers and grossing $1.6 trillion annually in the U.S. alone.

The key to success for **franchisers** is to replicate the business model with two or three local stores before expanding to faraway states or countries. The advantage to **franchisees** is that franchising reduces the risk of failure because the connect-the-dots business model has been successful in other locations. Unfortunately, in **franchising**, as in life, there are no guarantees. According to Jane Bryant Quinn, business writer for *Newsweek* magazine, 33% of franchises fail, 33% break even, and 33% make money.

To make matters worse, the average **franchise** requires $250,000 to get up and running, plus 3% to 6% of the gross monthly revenues. **Lodging franchises**, such as Holiday Inn, require the biggest initial investment, from $4 to $6 million, with restaurants right behind, costing $700,000 to $3.5 million. And that's just the start-up costs. Besides the monthly royalty payment, **franchise owners** often pay extra for advertising fees and must come out of pocket for equipment, maintenance, employees, insurance, mortgage or leasing payments, and inventory. Plus, you're likely locked into a long-term contract (10 years on average) even if the business is losing money.

Yes, **franchising** is a great way for the **franchisor** to take advantage of leverage, but with a success rate of only 33% and

> Today, franchising is a major contributor to the economies of the U.S. and Canada, accounting for 40 cents of every retail or service dollar spent in North America.

between $250,000 to $5 million in start-up costs, **franchisees** are the ones at risk.

Better to be the franchisor than the franchisee any day, wouldn't you agree?

Network Marketing: The "Personal Franchise"

Although the copycat format of **franchising** is an improvement on **traditional businesses**, only investors with deep pockets can afford the sky-high start-up costs and steep monthly licensing fees.

Great concept, **franchising**, but for a steep, steep price.

> While traditional businesses are struggling to compete in the global economy, business is booming in Network Marketing.

What if there were a **franchise-like concept** with all of the advantages of franchising at a fraction of the cost... a concept where you act like a franchisor and can earn royalties and commissions from your franchisees... a concept with a low cost of entry but a huge profit potential... a concept where you profit most by **leveraging** other people's time, efforts, and contacts... a concept with a 100-plus-year history that has doubled its revenues in the last decade but still has only 1% market penetration... a concept where top producers are rewarded for teaching and training you to become a success... a concept that taps into all four of the **Get R.E.A.L. and Get Rich** principles of wealth creation—**Recurring income, Equity, Appreciation,** and **Leverage**?

Well, there is such a concept. It's called **Network Marketing** (also known as **Referral Marketing... Relationship Marketing... Person-to-Person Marketing... Direct Selling... Personal Franchise...** or **Word-of Mouth Marketing**), and it's just getting geared up for the golden years ahead.

While **traditional businesses** are struggling to compete in the global economy, business is booming in **Network Marketing**. Turn the page to find out why.

Network Marketing: The Modern Method for Getting R.E.A.L. and Getting Rich

*Network Marketing is the first truly revolutionary
shift in modern marketing since Proctor & Gamble
over 50 years ago.*

—Tom Peters
world-renowned marketing expert

Okay, you've learned about the four key principles that rich people have used for centuries to get rich and stay rich—**Recurring income... Equity... Appreciation...** and **Leverage**.

So far you've learned about the **Museum Method** for getting rich, which is how you can create wealth by investing relatively small amounts of money over long periods of time. If you have 40 years to save and invest and the discipline to set aside three to four thousand dollars a year following the **ABCD plan**—**Automatic savings... Budgeting... Conservative investing...** and **Diversification**—then the **Museum Method** will make you a millionaire.

But what about people who want to **get R.E.A.L. and get rich** in four to five *years*... instead of four to five *decades*? How can they shrink the time frame so that they can *get rich and live rich during their 20s... 30s... 40s... and 50s,* instead of having to wait 40 or 50 years until retirement? What about people who want to live the American Dream all of their lives and not just in their waning years? How can they **get R.E.A.L. and get rich**?

The answer? The **Modern Method, also known as Network Marketing.**

> But what about people who want to get R.E.A.L. and get rich in four to five years... instead of four to five decades? How can they get R.E.A.L. and get rich? The answer? The Modern Method, also known as Network Marketing.

What Is Network Marketing?

Network Marketing is a form of distribution outside a fixed retail location. Network Marketers are independent contractors (referred to as independent business owners, reps, distributors, associates, or consultants) who partner with a manufacturer/wholesaler to market the company's products and services through **word-of-mouth**, the oldest and most powerful method of marketing.

Instead of paying out millions for traditional advertising, Network Marketing companies use that money to pay commissions and bonuses to the people marketing their products. Distributors can earn anywhere from a few hundred dollars per month by buying products at wholesale and selling at retail—to, in some cases, hundreds of thousands of dollars per month (yes, you read that right—PER MONTH) by recruiting and building a huge network of distributors and earning a percentage of the group's monthly sales volume.

Benefits to Both Parties

Both the parent company and the Network Marketer come out ahead in their partnership. The company gets to slash their advertising budget and replace it with a commission-only sales force, thereby reducing overhead and eliminating many of the costs of doing business. The company operates "lean and mean" because it doesn't pay salaries and benefits to middlemen—that is, jobbers, wholesalers, brokers, store managers, and clerks, or pay for satellite offices, phones, company cars, travel, and entertainment.

Little wonder, then, that *Fortune* magazine sang the praises of the industry with these words: "It's an investor's dream. The best-kept secret of the business world. An industry with steady annual growth... healthy cash flows... high return on invested capital... and long-term prospects for global expansion."

> The distributors are entitled to all of the benefits of owning their own franchise-type business without the huge start-up costs.

The distributors, on the other hand, are entitled to all of the benefits of owning their own franchise-type business without the huge start-up costs. Partnering with a parent company eliminates the need to deal with all of the expensive, aggravating, time-consuming back-office activities, such as product development... manufacturing... packaging... order taking... data processing... warehousing... shipping... research and development... finance... accounting... management... public relations... payroll... administration... and so on.

Because distributors don't have to deal with the time- and money-intensive "nuts and bolts of the business," it frees them to concentrate on talking to prospects and building their businesses.

And what a business it is! Just look at this list of advantages of working *for* yourself—but not *by* yourself—as a Network Marketing professional. Here are a few of the benefits that are attracting more and more people to this booming business:

- Be your own boss and set your own schedule
- Work from home, eliminating costly commutes
- Help yourself succeed by helping others succeed
- Low cost of entry with high-profit potential
- Choose the people you want to work with
- No glass ceiling and no limited territory
- Start making profits immediately
- Access to training from top-producing mentors

- Set your own goals and your own hours
- Work with motivated, positive people
- Plan your work around your life, not your life around work
- Franchise-like business means you copy a proven system
- Have fun, make friends, make money, and make a difference

Fortune 500 Companies Love Networking, Too

I'm not the only person other than distributors singing the praises of the industry. CEOs of Fortune 500 companies are either buying or starting up Network Marketing divisions to complement their marketing mix. Just look at a partial list of giant, long-established companies that own Network Marketing companies:

Citibank
Berkshire Hathaway (Warren Buffett's holding company)
Unilever
Sara Lee
Crayola
TimeWarner
The Body Shop
Reader's Digest

What makes dozens of CEOs worldwide and Warren Buffett, the world's second, richest man, so excited about the industry that he has bought three Network Marketing companies and calls his purchases "the best investment I ever made"?

> CEOs of Fortune 500 companies are either buying or starting up Network Marketing divisions to complement their marketing mix.

Four words: **word-of-mouth marketing**. Although **word-of-mouth marketing** has been around since the advent of speech, it's even more relevant and effective today than ever before. Research shows that consumers are turned off by traditional advertising. We've become numb to the constant barrage of annoying, intrusive advertising messages from TV, radio, billboards, newspapers, the Internet, cars, and trucks (and even bulletin boards in commercial restrooms).

Forrester Research reports that only 10% of consumers are influenced by TV ads... 9% by newspaper ads... and a lowly 6% by radio ads. By comparison, **56% of consumers say their buying decisions are strongly influenced by friends, family, and acquaintances.**

"We're in a new business era," says New York restaurateur Danny Meyer. "The service economy has given way to the **hospitality economy**. If you simply have a superior product and go through the motions of service, that's not enough. If you are devoted to your team and can promise them much more than a paycheck, *something to believe in,* then you will get the best people who give the best service for the customers."

> Network Marketing—it's the ultimate hospitality economy because it improves the quality of people's lives— financially... physically... socially... and personally.

Unbeknownst to Meyer, **Network Marketing** pioneered the **hospitality economy** with armies of passionate, dedicated distributors with "something to believe in"—a belief in the products... a belief in free enterprise... a belief in self-employment... a belief in the beauty of their dreams... a belief in their team and its mission to make a difference in people's lives by sharing one-of-a-kind quality products and services along with a business opportunity that can empower people to **get R.E.A.L. and get rich.**

Network Marketing—it's the ultimate **hospitality economy** because it improves the quality of people's lives—financially... physically... socially... and personally. Little wonder, then, that the industry has grown every single year for 20 consecutive years and doubled in the last 10 to $30 billion in the U.S. and $100 billion worldwide—and is positioned to continue to grow and prosper while traditional businesses are struggling to keep their doors open.

Getting R.E.A.L. and Getting Rich in Network Marketing

Okay, time to see how Network Marketing takes advantage of the **R.E.A.L. principles** of wealth creation and makes it the **Modern Method** of wealth creation and the best business for the 21st century.

In the previous chapters, we've learned how the rich have gotten rich and stayed rich for centuries through **Recurring income...** **Equity... Appreciation...** and **Leverage**. Now let's look at how **Network Marketing** exploits each of these principles and collapses the time it takes to get rich from many decades... to a few years.

Recurring Income

Recurring income, also called "residual income" or "passive income," results from **building pipelines** (do the work once and get paid again and again) as opposed to **carrying buckets** (trading time for money). **Recurring income** has long been the source of income for "creative types," such as songwriters, recording artists, and writers, who can earn a steady stream of revenue from royalties and licensing agreements.

If a novel or song becomes a classic, it can pump out millions of dollars of **Recurring income** each year for decades. For example, Elvis Presley died in 1977, but royalties from his songs, movies, and likeness generate $50 to $80 million a year. The classic novel *To Kill a Mockingbird* was first published in 1960, yet it continues to sell several hundred thousand copies a year, earning its reclusive author, Harper Lee, hundreds of thousands in annual royalties four decades after it was first released.

Few of us have the talent to write a hit song or bestselling book, but **Network Marketing** empowers virtually anyone with a high school education or above and a willingness to learn and work to create a stream of recurring income.

The key feature of **Network Marketing** that creates **Recurring income** is the franchise-like business model. Just as franchisers receive monthly royalties of 3% to 6% of gross revenues from all of their franchisees, Networkers receive a percentage of the entire gross volume of their organization. The more people you recruit, teach, and train... and the more people they recruit, teach, and train, the bigger your organization—and the bigger your pipeline, the bigger your paychecks.

There are literally thousands of **Network Marketing** professionals who've been enjoying **Recurring income** for decades! Just think—

wouldn't it be great to get monthly checks in the mail for 10 years… 20 years… 30 years or more? Best of all, the vast majority of Networking businesses are **sellable and willable assets**, which means your recurring income can be sold or transferred to your spouse and children when you pass. In Networking, there are instances of three generations receiving the benefits of **ongoing residual income**. Can't say that for most businesses, can you?

Equity

There are basically two ways to own your own business—you can *buy it*… or you can *build it*. Although most **Network Marketing** businesses can be bought and sold, just like any traditional business, most successful distributors build their businesses.

As we've discussed, the average **franchise** requires several hundred thousand dollars to get started, compared to several hundred dollars for the average **Network Marketing** business, a ridiculously small amount to pay for the right to own 100% of the **equity** in your own business.

> There are basically two ways to own your own business—you can buy it… or you can build it.

Consider this: Partners in successful law firms divide up the lion's share of the profits because they share in the **equity**. But to become partner, you first have to graduate from college… graduate from law school… pass the bar exam… and then labor 12 hours a day, six days a week for three to five years before even being considered as an equity partner. If you're talented and hard-working enough to be invited to become an equity partner, then you must "buy into the firm" by purchasing stock in the company, which entitles you to share in a percentage of the profits instead of just receiving a paycheck. **Equity** positions in small firms in small cities can cost more than $100,000. **Equity** partnerships in premier firms in major cities can run five to 10 times that amount.

Let's see—do you want to borrow and invest $100,000 to $1 million to own 5% to 10% of a law firm, accounting firm, or physician's practice? Or invest $100 to $200 out of your pocket to own 100% of your own **Network Marketing** business? That's a no-brainer if there ever was one.

We've already discussed many of the benefits of owning your own business, such as being your own boss and setting your own hours. But as the authors of *The Millionaire Next Door* discovered, **66% of millionaires in the U.S. are self-employed** and 20% of the average millionaire's total net worth is tied up in their business, which tells me **owning a business is the best way to get R.E.A.L. and get rich.**

The question isn't whether you should own your own business. The question is which business gives you the biggest return on your investment in the least amount of time. My answer is **Network Marketing**.

Appreciation

As your **Network Marketing** organization gets larger, it **appreciates** in value. But unlike traditional franchises which **grow linearly** (1 + 1 = 2), your **Networking** business **grows exponentially** 1 + 1 = 4), which forces **appreciation** at warp speed.

How can 1 + 1 = 4? Through the magic of **exponential growth** in **Network Marketing**. Exponential growth takes advantage of the **doubling concept** we talked about in Chapter 5 on **Appreciation**, except in **Network Marketing**, the numbers double in months, instead of years.

> Unlike traditional franchises which grow linearly (1 + 1 = 2), your Networking business grows exponentially (1 + 1 = 4), which forces appreciation at warp speed.

The easiest way to explain the power of the **doubling concept** is to ask people to answer this simple question: What would you prefer to have, a penny doubled every day for a month or $10,000 in cash?

Most people would settle for $10,000 without so much as a second thought. And the returns in the early part of the month would indicate that taking the $10,000 upfront would the best deal. After five days of doubling a penny, you'd have all of 16 cents.

After 15 days, halfway to the end, you'd only have $163.84. But the real **power of the doubling concept** occurs on the back side. On day 25, you'd have $167,000. The next day it would double to $335,000. The next to $671,000—and you still have 3 days of doubling left. Which means by the end of 30 days, **a penny a day doubled would calculate to more than $5 million!**

This same **doubling concept** is what powers **Network Marketing**—and has distributors, as well as seasoned CEOs, hyperventilating with excitement. Follow along as I show you how **exponential growth** can make your business—and your net worth—explode in months and years, instead of having to wait decades.

Imagine that you've just started your own Networking business. Do you think you could find just one other person each month to join your business? One person a month is all it takes to get you on your way to **getting R.E.A.L. and getting rich**.

In month one, you "sponsor" one person to join you in your business (to keep the calculation simple, we'll add just one new person each month), and you teach your new partner to do the same—sponsor just one good person a month. So, by the end of month one, your organization looks like this:

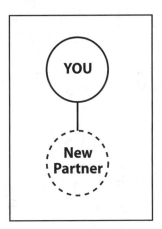

Month two, your new person sponsors one person, while you sponsor another, so now you have **doubled** to a group of four—you plus three others.

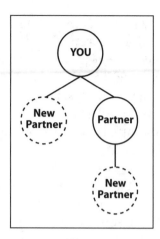

Each of you does the same for months three, four, five, and so on through 12 months, **doubling** each month. At the end of the first year, you'll have personally sponsored just 12 people and each one of those people will have sponsored just one person a month, and so on down the line. Yet, due to the awesome power of the **doubling concept**, at the end of your first year in the business, *you'd have 4,096 people in your organization!*

With hyper-dynamic numbers like that, it's not hard to see why Fortune 500 companies are jumping on the **Network Marketing** bandwagon.

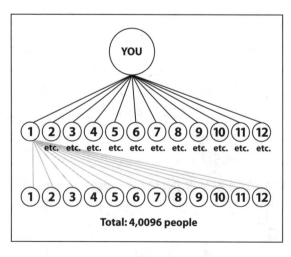

Leverage

Leverage is most often associated with using **OPM**—other people's money. **OPM** is what makes it possible for middle-class people to own a home and buy rental properties. By putting 10% down, you can **leverage** 90% of the purchase with a mortgage while receiving 100% of the benefits of owning real estate.

But because the cost of entry into **Network Marketing** is so ridiculously low compared to traditional businesses, your Networking business will be built around leveraging other people's time, efforts, and contacts, rather than leveraging **OPM**.

J. Paul Getty, the multi-billionaire investor, best described the **power of leveraging** other people's time and efforts with these words: "I'd rather have 1% of 100 men's efforts than 100% of my own." Network Marketing is a perfect example of Getty's axiom in action. You can only be one place at one time. If you spend two hours an evening working your business, five days a week, that adds up to 10 hours of time and effort each week. But if you had 100 people in your organization doing the same, you'd **leverage** your time and efforts to 200 hours a night (2 hours x 100 people) and 1,000 hours a week (200 hours x 5 days).

Leveraging Other People's Time and Efforts

One person	100 people
2 hours a night	2 hours a night
5 nights a week	5 nights a week
10 hours a week	**1,000 hours a week**

Every **traditional business** owner understands the principle of **leveraging money** (that's why they get loans from banks and family members) and **leveraging their time and efforts** (that's why they hire employees).

But with the exception of top-producing insurance and real estate agents, few business owners understand how to leverage **OPC**—other people's contacts. **Network Marketing**, on the other hand, turns **contacts into capital**. Going back to our earlier example of leverage, if you have 100 people in your organization working two hours a day, five days a week... and if each of those people contacts just 10 people a week, through **leverage**, you'd be making 10,000 contacts a week.

Leveraging Other People's Contacts	
100 people 2 hours a night 5 nights a week	1,000 hours a week 10 contacts
1,000 hours a week	**10,000 contacts a week**

Modern Method vs. the Museum Method

Are you beginning to see how **Network Marketing** uses **leverage** to maximize other people's time... efforts... and contacts? Unlike the **Museum Method** of wealth creation, which takes decades to create financial independence, Network Marketing's hyper-dynamic business model compresses time into months and years, instead of decades, making it the perfect **Modern Method** for getting rich... and staying rich.

> Network Marketing's hyper-dynamic business model compresses time into months and years, instead of decades, making it the perfect Modern Method for getting rich... and staying rich.

Don't get me wrong—I'm not knocking the **Museum Method**. Better to build wealth patiently over decades than to end up depending on Social Security because you frittered away your assets. That's why I recommend you DO BOTH! To quote once again the author of *Who Stole the American Dream?*, Burke Hedges: "Live for today, plan for tomorrow."

Building a successful Network Marketing business with the **Modern Method** is *living for today.*

Using the **ABCD plan (Automatic savings... Budgeting... Conservative Investments... Diversificatioin)** to save and invest wisely over time with the **Museum Method** is *planning for tomorrow.* Employing both the **Museum Method** and the **Modern Method** means you can *live rich...* and *retire rich.*

That's an American Dream no one can steal from you.

Chapter 8

Get R.E.A.L. and Get Richer by Paying Less Tax!

I'm proud to pay taxes in the United States. The only thing is, I could be just as proud for half the money.
—Arthur Godfrey,
American entertainer

Everywhere you turn, the tax man has his hand out.

Income taxes... Social Security and Medicare taxes... property taxes... utility taxes... phone taxes... sales taxes... gas taxes... local taxes... state taxes... county taxes... license plate taxes... intangible taxes... estate taxes... capital gains taxes... and transportation taxes, to name a few.

Whew! Today, more than ever before, people are taxed to the max!

Like most Americans, I can't say I *like* paying taxes. But I honestly believe that paying taxes is more than a fair trade off, given the benefits I get from living in this country. And I honestly believe that most Americans feel the same way I do.

Yes, we may grumble when we see our property tax bill go up every year. And we may cringe each time we look at our paycheck stubs and notice how much of our hard-earned money is withheld for taxes. But the vast majority of Americans recognize that taxes are a relatively small price to pay for the large privilege of living and working in the U.S.A.

Who Pays Most of the Income Tax in the U.S.?

Politicians are always talking about income taxes. Some politicians say income taxes are too high for the poor and middle-class people. Others argue taxes are too low for rich people. Truth is, our income tax code is so complex, few of us even know who is paying what. So, I've prepared a chart based on Internal Revenue Service data to show you who's *really* paying to keep U.S.A. Inc. up and running. The findings will shock and amaze you.

First, the facts: In 2005, there were 132 million tax returns filed. The IRS reports that 79 million of those returns paid taxes. **That leaves 53 million, or 40% of all filers, who paid zero income taxes.**

> If you're in the top 50% of wage earners in this country, you're paying income taxes for at least one other person, who gets a free pass.

Think about that for a moment—*4 out of every 10 workers in the U.S. does not pay a single dime in income tax.* Another 23 million workers pay only 3.3% of the tax bill, which means 66 million income tax payers—that's *fully 50% of all taxpayers— pay just 3.3% of our income taxes every year.* Which means if you're in the top 50% of wage earners in this country, you're paying income taxes for at least one other person, who gets a free pass.

The best way to explain who is *really* paying income tax is for you to imagine 100 people representing a cross section of the American taxpayers standing outside the U.S. Treasury waiting to pay their portion of the income taxes collected for the year. Here's a breakdown of the percentage of the federal income tax bill each of these Americans is responsible for:

Cross Section of 100 American Taxpayers

Income	% of Income Tax Paid Each Year
40 lowest-paid workers	**Pay 0%**
10 next-lowest-paid workers	**Pay 3.3%**

Summary: Bottom 50% pay 3.3%
Top 50 pay 96.70%

1 highest-paid worker*	**Pays 37%**
5 highest-paid workers	**Pay 54%**
10 highest-paid workers**	**Pay 70%**

Top 1% earn average of $137.000
**Top 10% earn average of $87,000 a year*

Summary: Top earners are taxed to the max

There are a whole bunch of people who would love to earn $87,000 a year, but that's hardly the income of a rich person. Yet 70% of the income tax collected to operate and defend our country is coming from millions of households earning less than $90,000 a year.

Seems pretty out of whack, doesn't it?

So, the next time somebody starts whining about "tax breaks for the rich," just point out the statistics from the above chart. Rich people—of which I'm proud to be one—pay plenty of income tax, that's for sure.

But you know what—I consider myself fortunate to be one of the top 1% who shoulders nearly 40% of the tax bill. No, I don't want to overpay my taxes. But I'm more than willing to write a check to the IRS in accordance to their tax guidelines. I say that because I was born Cuba, and if my dad hadn't had the courage to get us out, today I'd be working in Cuba for state wages.

Know how much a state worker in Cuba earns each month? $15.

You read that right—*the average state worker in Cuba makes $15 a month.*

Why Volunteer to Overpay Your Taxes?

Considering I could be living in Cuba on $15 a month, the income taxes I pay annually to the U.S. government don't seem so burdensome.

You won't catch me whining and moaning every April 15.

Although I have no objections to paying my allotted share of income taxes, that doesn't mean I'm interested in OVERPAYING my taxes. And neither should you. No one is obligated to pay an unfair share by OVERPAYING their taxes.

> There are only two rules when it comes to paying taxes.
> **Rule One:** *Don't cheat the government.*
> **Rule Two:** *Don't cheat yourself, either.*

But amazingly, more than half of all taxpayers do just that—*they voluntarily overpay their federal income tax.* According to *USA Today*, tens of millions of U.S. citizens OVERPAY more than a BILLION in federal income taxes every year, which calculates to an average of $438 per household. Could you use an extra $438 a year TAX FREE? Who couldn't, especially in today's economic environment?

The way I see it, there are only two rules when it comes to paying taxes.

Rule One: *Don't cheat the government.*

Rule Two: *Don't cheat yourself, either.*

Very few people break **Taxpayer's Rule One** because the penalty for cheating on your income taxes is, at best, stiff fines plus 18% interest on unpaid taxes… or, at worst, jail time PLUS a stiff fine. But 100 million people voluntarily break **Taxpayer's Rule Two: Don't cheat yourself, either.** Why? Because they're choosing to take the standard deductions instead of itemizing. It seems that taxpayers are either so confused by the tax code or so fearful of an IRS audit that they opt to file the short form rather than itemize legitimate deductions.

Problem is, 100 million people who file the short form are cheating themselves by letting the IRS keep money that's legally theirs. Like most people, you wouldn't think of cheating the IRS, would you? Of course not! *Then why cheat yourself?*

Corporations Pay Less as You Pay More

While most individuals are overpaying their taxes, corporations are paying less income tax than ever before! Consider this. In 1940, companies and individuals each paid about 50% of the federal income tax. Today, companies pay 13.7%, *while individuals pay a whopping 86.3% of the federal tax bill!*

> Increasingly in Corporate America, the tax department has become a profit center. The reason is simple. At the current corporate tax rate of 35%, for every $1 worth of deductions, 35 cents stays in the company coffers.

Why the drop in corporate taxes? Because corporations have come to realize that tax savings go right to the company's bottom line, so they've cooked up all kinds of ways to avoid paying taxes. According to *Business Week* magazine, "Increasingly in Corporate America, the tax department has become a profit center." The reason is simple. At the current corporate tax rate of 35%, for every $1 worth of deductions, 35 cents stays in the company coffers. Thanks to brutal global competition, profit margins are getting skinnier and skinnier these days, so it doesn't take a financial wizard to see why CEOs get excited about a profit margin of 35 cents, does it?

It Pays to Itemize Deductions

Let me see if I've got this straight. *Cash-rich companies are saving tens of billions* each year by taking advantage of every available tax deduction... while *cash-poor individuals are overpaying a billion* each year by refusing to take all of the deductions they're entitled to.

Hey, don't you think it's time to wake up your inner accountant and claim the money that is rightfully yours? Look, it's one thing

Cash-rich companies are saving tens of billions each year, while cash-poor individuals are overpaying a billion each year by refusing to take all of the deductions they're entitled to.

for people to leave money on the table every year for the IRS to pick up. Some people will justify their decision by saying it's worth a few hundred dollars a year to know they'll never have to worry about being audited.

But what if that few hundred dollars turned into a few thousand dollars? (Over a 10-year period, that adds up to $20,000 or more—serious money in anybody's book.) Better yet, what if there were a way to save those thousands of dollars a year in only a few minutes a day—would that make itemizing sound a bit more appealing? Would a couple thousand extra dollars a year for a couple minutes of bookkeeping a day be enough of an incentive for you to stop breaking **Taxpayer's Rule Two—don't cheat yourself, either—**and keep all of the money that is rightfully yours?

Well, that's exactly what can happen when you commit yourself to itemizing the deductions you're legally entitled to while you're building your **Network Marketing business.** You see, as a self-employed business owner, you're eligible for **dozens of income tax deductions** that employed people aren't legally entitled to. And, if properly documented, these tax deductions can save you thousands of dollars a year.

Tax Breaks for Business Owners

There are two tax systems in this country—one for **employees** and another for **business owners.** Employees get short-changed TWICE because one, they make less money than employers; and two, they get fewer tax deductions. Business owners get the best of both worlds—they get to *make more money*, and they get to *keep more money* because they're entitled to numerous tax deductions that are unavailable to ordinary employees!

In effect, the government is paying you to become a business owner, and the moment you sign up as an associate with a **Network**

Marketing company, you automatically qualify as an independent business owner, making you legally eligible for dozens of tax deductions.

Now, I'm not suggesting you start a business just so you can get tax deductions. Let's be clear about this—the biggest reason to start a business is to make a profit, period! Think of business owners and the U.S. Treasury as riders on an economic merry-go-round that benefits both parties. The U.S. government uses tax deductions as an incentive to encourage more people to go into business for themselves which, in turn, generates more profits that can be taxed by the government. Becoming an independent business owner is a win/win proposition—business owners get tax breaks unavailable to employees and the government gets more tax revenues.

If documented properly, legitimate tax deductions can save you thousands of dollars a year in federal income taxes. For example, as a new business owner, you're entitled to deduct expenses related to building and running your business, which would include deductions for your car payment... gasoline... lunches and dinners with prospects... as well as tickets to sporting events and concerts... travel... business-related vacations... clothing with your company logo... education and training materials... conventions and live events... office equipment and supplies (including computers, cell phones, printers, etc.)... medical insurance premiums... PLUS a home office (including the carpet, drapes, office supplies, and even a portion of your heat and electric bill).

> There are two tax systems in this country—one for employees and another for business owners.

The key to your receiving credit for all these deductions, and many others, is to make sure all of your deductions are well-documented and conform to IRS guidelines. That's it—that's all there is to it.

There are even some little-known business deductions that, under the right circumstances, can save you thousands more in taxes. For example, you can pay each of your children from ages 7 to 18 up to $4,000 a year each TAX FREE for working in your business, while deducting their wages from your own tax bill. And, if you buy a new truck or SUV weighing more than 6,000 pounds and use it for transportation to build your business, you can immediately depreciate as much as $24,000 from the price of your new vehicle, PLUS 30% of the rest of the cost, which could easily calculate to saving $20,000 or more on the purchase of, say, a brand new Range Rover. *Amazing... but true!* Of course, detailed documentation is required and rules and restrictions apply, so check with your accountant to see if you would qualify.

The Hobby/Loss Rule

Now, does this mean that in order to receive these great tax deductions that the IRS requires you to quit your salaried job and work your new business full time? Nope. The government treats part-time business owners the same as full-timers. When you think about it, this is a smart move on the government's part because some of the biggest businesses in the world started with a person with a full-time dream working their business part time. (Does the name Michael Dell of Dell Computers ring a bell? How about Henry Ford? Both started as part-time entrepreneurs.)

> Now, does this mean that in order to receive these great tax deductions that the IRS requires you to quit your salaried job and work your new business full time? Nope. The government treats part-time business owners the same as full-timers.

Although the IRS doesn't distinguish between part-time and full-time business owners, the agency DOES require part-timers to demonstrate two things: One, they have to actively work in their business to qualify for business deductions. And two, they have to pursue a profit.

Now, notice I said "pursue" a profit, not MAKE a profit. It's not unusual for a new business to lose money while getting off the ground. And, yes, some profitable businesses hit rough periods during which they lose money until they right the ship. But according to IRS guidelines known as the "Hobby/Loss Rule," your business must have a plan to make money and show a profit three out of five years in order to be classified as a true business. Otherwise, you run the risk of having the IRS classify your business as a hobby, and, thus, you may be faced with paying a fine and penalties for all of the expenses they disallow.

If You Don't Know Jewelry, Know the Jeweler

In 1913, when the income tax was added to the U.S. Constitution, the federal tax code was 400 pages long, which is about the size of a small-town phone book. Today, the official U.S. income tax code is 54,846 pages, which, stacked on the floor, would reach 16 feet in height! It's no mystery why major corporations employ a small army of tax lawyers and accountants to decipher our tax code, which grows in complexity and volume every year.

> It would be money well spent for you to schedule a two-hour meeting with your accountant to learn about the deductions you're entitled to as an active Network Marketer and the best way to document them.

Fortunately, you don't have to know the tax code inside and out—all you have to do is know an accountant who does. As Warren Buffett, the world's most successful stock market investor, says, "If you don't know jewelry, know the jeweler." Likewise, if you don't know the tax laws, know an accountant who does. Trust me on this one—it would be money well spent for you to schedule a two-hour meeting with your accountant to learn about the deductions you're entitled to as an active **Network Marketer** and the best way to document them.

Document! Document! Document!

I don't pretend to be a tax expert, but I can tell you this much about the tax code. As far as the IRS is concerned, documentation is more important than the deductions themselves. Without proper documentation, your business deductions—even if they're perfectly legitimate—can end up costing you 10 times the amount of the

> As far as the IRS is concerned, documentation is more important than the deductions themselves.

deduction. Why? Because when the IRS disallows a deduction, you not only owe taxes on the deduction, you may also owe penalties and interest on the disallowed deductions.

How to Turn Minutes into Money

Let me ask you a question. Would you be willing to spend two minutes a day to earn $2,000 a year? Think about it—two minutes a day... that calculates to about 15 minutes a week... which is an hour a month... or 12 hours a year. Divide 12 hours a year into $2,000, and you get $167 AN HOUR tax free! That's the kind of return on your time that you can get from itemizing legitimate business deductions.

Now are you beginning to see the advantages of itemizing?

Look, I realize that keeping track of every little receipt and entering your mileage to and from business meetings into a mileage log is a nuisance. But when you look at the trade-off—perhaps a couple thousand dollars a year for a couple minutes a day—well, in my opinion, anyone who isn't willing to put up with a little aggravation for that kind of money deserves to lose it.

Believe me—I'm anything but a bookkeeper-type person. But over the years, I've come up with a simple system for itemizing expenses, and it has saved me tens of thousands of dollars in taxes. Because different people have different styles, I'm going to describe three basic systems for documenting your **Network Marketing business expenses**. At one time or the other, I've used all three systems in my business, so I know they all work. But all three systems require you to keep a day timer or journal of your business-related meetings, keep a mileage log of your business driving, and keep receipts for all of your expenses

Three Systems: Daily, Monthly, and Yearly

Most people's lives are so hectic that they have to use a daytimer to keep track of their schedules anyway, so for most people, keeping a daily appointment book isn't anything new. But just to be safe, you may want to keep a little more detail in your appointment book than you're used to. For example, if you expand the entry "Lunch with Joe" to "Joe Landis. Lunch at Frank's Deli. Discussed opportunity," then that should satisfy the IRS.

Whichever system you choose to use doesn't really matter—you either "pay now" by keeping daily records or "pay later" by organizing all of your expenses at the end of the year. You know yourself best, so choose the system that works best for you.

Two-Minutes-a-Day System

Buy a dozen manila folders or an accordion file. Label each file according to the deduction, such as "Lunches & Dinners," "Car Expenses," "Office Supplies & Equipment," and so on. Each time you make a purchase for your business, write on the receipt in ink the type of purchase and the purpose. Then toss the receipt into the proper folder.

One-Hour-a-Month System

Buy a plastic pouch that fits into your planner. (If you don't own a planner, buy one—today!) Each time you make a purchase, jot down what it was and the purpose, and toss it into the pouch. At the end of the month, when you're paying bills or going over your credit card statement, sort your expenses into #10 envelopes, add up the amount in each envelope, and write the total on the back.

One-Weekend-a-Year System

Also called the "Shoebox Filing System." All you need are three or four empty shoeboxes labeled according to the biggest categories of expenses: "Business Credit Card," "Cash Expenses," "Lunches and Dinners," and "Odds and Ends." Each time you incur an expense, write down the purpose and toss it into the appropriate shoebox. This is a virtually pain-free way to keep track of your daily expenses, but the downside is that you have to set aside a day or two in December

> To maximize the profits in your Network Marketing business, remember these simple rules.
>
> Keep working your business.
>
> Keep good records.
>
> And then keep more money in your household, right where it belongs!

to organize all of your expenses. As I said earlier, "Pay now or pay later," right?

Small Pain, Big Gain!

Yes, keeping receipts, logs, and records is a nuisance, but considering the money you can SAVE—money that is rightfully and legally YOURS—it's time and effort well spent. So, to maximize the profits in your **Network Marketing** business, remember these simple rules.

Keep working your business.

Keep good records.

And then keep more money in your household, *right where it belongs*!

The Millionaire Mentality

A man can only rise, conquer, and achieve by lifting up his thoughts.

—James Allen
from *As a Man Thinketh*

You find wisdom in the unlikeliest places, as a friend of mine was recently reminded.

My friend was in the barbershop getting a haircut when he and the female stylist started talking about TV. They were both laughing about the tendency of men to turn on the television as soon as they got home from work and then watching it until they fell asleep on the couch.

"You know why men watch so much TV, don't you?" she asked.

"Not really," my friend said.

"So they don't have to think," she replied.

Thinking Is Hard Work

I hate to admit it, but the stylist is right. We don't have to think when we watch television because the TV does the thinking for us, which is real scary when you, um, *think* about it.

Thinking is what sets us apart from the other animals, yet we go to great lengths to avoid it because, as Henry Ford observed, "Thinking is the hardest work there is, which is probably why so few engage in it." Actually, when Ford said thinking is hard work, he was talking about positive, **productive thinking,** which is, indeed, hard work.

It's hard work, for example, to think of creative solutions to complex problems.

It's hard work to think positive thoughts while being bombarded by negative messages.

It's hard work to think good things about ourselves instead of replaying "old, negative scripts" that remind us we aren't capable... aren't deserving... and aren't worthy.

But if you're serious about **getting R.E.A.L. and getting rich,** first you have to think like rich people think. And rich people think positive, self-affirming thoughts that keep them centered and focused on making the choices that lead to financial independence.

Strangest Secret Isn't So Strange

When I first started on my quest for financial independence, I took to heart the advice of my mentor, Tom Murphy, when he told me to become a student of positive thinking.

"If you're not getting the results you want," he told me, "let go of your life-defeating thoughts. Think success. Once you do, you'll never again submit to failure."

> Nightingale's message was simple yet powerful: You become what you think about.

Among the many audio programs Murphy recommended was *The Strangest Secret,* Earl Nightingale's classic recording and the only spoken-word record to earn a gold record for selling more than a million copies. Nightingale's message was simple yet powerful: **You become what you think about.** Nightingale believed that success was nothing more than energy in an orderly state. Conversely, failure was disorderly energy. So, he devised a simple formula for success:

positive thoughts = positive feelings = positive actions = outstanding results

Now, I want you to know that it wasn't easy for me to reprogram myself to think positive thoughts. After all, my early life was dominated by more negative experiences than positive ones. Up until the time I met Murphy, I was an insecure college dropout and failed singer earning less than minimum wage while living in a 200-square-foot studio apartment.

Not a lot of positives to focus on, wouldn't you agree?

But I kept reading positive books and listening to positive audios, and, gradually, I started replacing negative thoughts with positive ones. Sure enough, I started to see changes in my life, and within six months of meeting Murphy, I moved up from last in sales at my health club to the number one salesperson.

I was on my way to **getting R.E.A.L. and getting rich!**

Erasing Negative Thoughts

If you're sincere about improving your finances, you have to start by improving your thinking. James Allen, author of the seminal book on positive thinking, *As a Man Thinketh*, likens the mind to a garden:

"Just as a gardener cultivates his plot, keeping it free from weeds and growing the flowers and fruits which he requires, so may a man tend the garden of his mind, weeding out the wrong, useless, and impure thoughts and cultivating toward perfection the flowers and fruits of right, useful, and pure thoughts."

Like weeds in a garden, negative thoughts keep popping up from time to time because the seeds (which were planted in our minds years ago) lie dormant in our subconscious until one day, *boing*, a handful of negative thoughts springs to life, threatening to choke out the positive thoughts. As the gardener, it's your job to dig up the negative thoughts and replant healthy, positive thoughts in their place.

One of the ways to do that is a technique I call **Effective Erasing**. Whenever a negative thought enters my mind, I imagine the most awful scratching noise, like a needle being dragged back and forth across a spinning record. That imagined sound reminds me to erase the negative thought and replace it with a positive one.

I encourage you to think of your own **Effective Eraser.** A friend of mine imagines the sound of a garbage truck backing up to empty a garbage can containing his negative thoughts. Another friend imagines the sound of fingernails clawing down a blackboard, followed by a giant eraser wiping away the negative thought. The key is to think of a sound and an image that eliminates the negative thought.

> The most stubborn weed of negativity is called excuses.

Sounds corny, but it works.

Excuses: The Hardest Weeds to Kill

Just as there are hundreds of hardy weeds in a garden, some are harder to get rid of than others. Same goes for negative thoughts, and the most stubborn weed of negativity is called **excuses**.

We're all prone to **excuse making** because excuses allow us to rationalize our failures. Excuses are weeds because they encourage us to **give in and give up**, instead of remaining positive and thinking of ways to overcome obstacles. People generally make excuses in one of the following seven areas:

Excuse #	Self-Talk
#1 **Fear of Failure**	"I won't try because I might fail."
#2 **Pain of Change**	"I'm not comfortable doing that."
#3 **Self Doubt**	"I'm not very good at (fill in the blank)."
#4 **Blaming Others**	"Mistakes were made by (blank)."
#5 **Justifying**	"Everybody cuts corners, so I did, too."
#6 **Complaining**	"The problem is (company, products, etc.)."
#7 **Lack of Skills**	"I've never been able to talk to people."

Excuses might make you feel better in the short run, but in the long run, they won't help you **get R.E.A.L. and get rich.** For every excuse people can come up with for NOT getting rich, I can give five examples of people who have triumphed in the face of worse circumstances.

> You can make excuses or you can make money. You just can't do both at the same time.

"You can make excuses or you can make money," goes the old saying. "You just can't do both at the same time." So true.

It's like I tell my audiences—every diet works, and every diet doesn't work. The common denominator for losing weight is the dieter, not the diet. Lance Armstrong, cancer survivor and seven-time Tour de France winner, expressed the same sentiment by choosing a no-excuses title for his best-selling autobiography: *It's Not About the Bike*.

The Millionaire DNA

I believe that all North Americans have the potential to amass great wealth. It's stamped in our DNA. I'm not saying that just to pump you up. Our DNA is literally designed to facilitate our **getting R.E.A.L. and getting rich**.

In a recent book titled *The Hypomanic Edge*, psychologist John D. Gartner theorizes that the main reason North America has become so rich and powerful lies in our genes. We're a nation of entrepreneurs, Dr. Gartner argues, because we were mostly populated by immigrants who had the will, optimism, and daring to take a leap into the unknown and seek fame, fortune, and freedom in a foreign country.

From our immigrant ancestors we inherited **hypomania**, a mild form of mania that endows us with unusual energy, creativity, enthusiasm, and a propensity for taking risks.

Statistics indicate Dr. Gartner's theory has a basis in fact. Since the 1970s, America has created 60 million new jobs, compared to just four million in Europe, where most of those jobs are in government. In 2006, a record number of Americans started companies—nearly 700,000 new companies with employees were created and perhaps three times that many sole proprietorships. Each year, North Americans start up twice as many businesses as England and three times more than the rest of Europe.

> We're a nation of entrepreneurs, Dr. Gartner argues, because we were mostly populated by immigrants who had the will, optimism, and daring to take a leap into the unknown.

"It's not easy to recreate the success of Silicon Valley," says Bjoern Christensen, a Dane now managing a software company in California. "The U.S. start-up culture is like generations of people where the gene pool gets better and better. *The magic is in the DNA.*"

I call it the **Millionaire DNA**, and it gives each of us the edge to **get R.E.A.L. and get rich.** All humans are built to create—it's wired into our brains. And as the result of welcoming immigrants from all over the world, North America is populated by a collection of the world's boldest and brightest, which gives us an edge when it comes to making money... making things... and making a difference.

What's Holding You Back?

If we're descended from opportunity seekers, wealth creators, and business builders, why aren't more of us getting rich? Why are so many of us deep in debt... denying our **Millionaire DNA** by staying in jobs where we're overworked and underpaid?

The answer is in our flawed thinking.

The **Millionaire Mentality** is based on the **Law of Attraction**—whatever we think about, we attract. If we think about success and wealth, success and wealth will follow. If we think about failure and debt, failure and debt will follow.

The **Law of Attraction** is the mental variation of the **Law of Cause and Effect:** We sow with our thoughts, and then we reap the reality those thoughts bring about. If we think about creating wealth and harmony in our lives, we will **attract** people, opportunities, and circumstances that manifest wealth and harmony.

> The Millionaire Mentality is based on the Law of Attraction—whatever we think about, we attract.

So it follows, if you want grow your wealth, you have to sow thoughts that attract wealth. If you want to **get R.E.A.L. and get rich**, you have to sow thoughts that will attract people, opportunities, information, and circumstances that will deliver **Recurring income... Equity... Appreciation...** and **Leverage** into your life, which will then cause you to become rich.

I tell my audiences that getting rich starts in your **think account,** and ends up in your **bank account**. I started making a ton of money before I started getting rich because I was spending every dime I made.

> Getting rich starts in your think account and ends up in your bank account.

The money was coming in but the correct thoughts weren't going out to the world, so the money was disappearing as fast as I got it. Once I changed from thinking about how to acquire more "bling" that **depreciated** and made me poorer—like new cars and new clothes... to thinking about how to acquire more assets that **appreciated** and made me richer—like real estate, businesses, and IRAs—then I started getting rich.

I'm living proof that if you change your thinking, you can change your life.

And so can you!

Change from minimum-wage mentality... to **Millionaire Mentality...** and you'll be on your way to **getting R.E.A.L. and getting rich**.

How to Pass the Test

*I count a man who overcomes his desires braver
than a man who conquers his enemies; the hardest
victory is victory over self.*

—Aristotle

I'd like to end with a powerful story about what can happen when you choose to fulfill your obligations instead of giving in to temptations. If you have the wisdom to grasp the moral of this story and the discipline and integrity to make the right choices day in and day out, then you'll be well on your way to **getting R.E.A.L. and getting rich**.

Here's the story.

Some Kind of Test

A Love Story

December 11, 1945. Nervously pacing in front of the information booth at New York's Grand Central Station, a young uniformed soldier scans the crowd of Christmas shoppers as they hurry through the terminal. The soldier studies the overcoats of each passing woman, hoping to see a red rose in a lapel that will identify her as the woman he had exchanged hundreds of letters with during the course of the war.

He grips the book he has carried with him throughout the long campaigns in North Africa and Europe.

"Well, Mr. Donne," the soldier thinks to himself as he glances at the threadbare spine of *The Poetry of John Donne*, "we'll soon see—to use your words—'if the woman be constant.'"

The woman he is referring to is what the movies would call "the mystery woman," for they haven't met in person, their only contact being a steady stream of letters during the last four years.

Today is the long-awaited day they finally meet face to face.

"Meet me on December 11, at four p.m., in front of the information desk in Grand Central Station," she wrote in her last letter. "Wear your uniform and carry our favorite book. I'll have a red rose in my coat lapel. We'll have dinner and catch up on our lives. Until then, I suffer to think I'm being foolish, for John Donne's words haunt my thoughts: "I am two fools, I know, for loving and for saying so."

The soldier recognizes her parting words as the opening lines to Donne's poem *The Triple Fool*. He whispers to himself, "It's only fitting that she sign off with Donne, for it was Donne who brought us together in the first place."

# # #

Their story begins in early December of 1941. Looking to kill time on furlough, the soldier wanders into a used bookstore. He gravitates to the literature section before zeroing in on poetry, calculating that it would be easier for him to read short poems in his spare moments during active duty.

He pulls *The Poetry of John Donne* from the top shelf and opens the book to one of Donne's sonnets, "Woman's Constancy." He scans the opening stanza:

Now thou hast loved me one whole day,
Tomorrow when thou leavest, what wilt thou say?

In the margin is a comment written in a tight, graceful cursive:

Just another insecure man looking to break it off before he gets his feelings hurt.

The soldier smiles at the sharp insight. As he thumbs through the book, he discovers that every page is filled with clever comments in the same tight cursive. Enchanted by the reader's notes as much as the poetry, the soldier buys the book and heads for the park, where he spends the afternoon reading and rereading the poems of John Donne and the comments from the anonymous reader.

He discovers the previous owner's name and hometown inscribed on the inside front cover. Upon returning to his military base, he enlists the help of some fellow soldiers in communications and finds the woman's address. That evening, the soldier writes the woman a letter introducing himself and asking if they could meet in person.

The next day fate intervenes once more. Pearl Harbor is attacked, and America officially enters WWII. The young soldier is shipped to North Africa, then to Italy and France until the war comes to a close in the spring of 1945. The soldier and his mystery woman continue writing weekly during the four years he's at war, and, not surprisingly, the letters become increasingly intimate, and the word "love" is shared by both letter writers.

The handsome young soldier includes photographs in some of his letters, but each time he requests her photo, she refuses, arguing that inner beauty is the only true, enduring beauty, and she quotes their beloved Donne to prove her point:

But he who loveliness within
Hath found, all outward loathes;
For he who color loves, and skin,
Loves but their oldest clothes.

So, as the war ends and the world returns to civilian matters, the lovelorn soldier finds himself pacing in front the information desk at Grand Central Station, eager and intrigued to finally meet his mystery woman, but anxious and nervous that the outer beauty of his unseen love will be incompatible with her inner beauty.

"I don't expect, nor need, a dazzling beauty," he thinks to himself as he studies a parade of coat lapels for a red rose. "But her reluctance to send her photo makes me more than a bit apprehensive about her appearance."

Suddenly, the soldier sees a stunning young woman with a bright, warm smile walking toward him. She's easily the most beautiful woman he's ever seen in person.

She approaches him straight on, tilts her head to the side, and says, "Soldier, you look a little cold and a lot lost. Can I buy you a cup of coffee and help you get your bearings in the big city?"

As the blushing soldier searches for a reply, he glances at her coat lapel, hoping to see a red rose. The lapel is empty.

"I'd love to take you up on your offer," he stutters. "But I'm supposed to meet someone. Sorry, but I'll have to pass."

As the woman turns on her heel to leave, the young man is tempted to reconsider, but decides to honor his commitment. He watches as she fades into the moving sea of coats. He turns back to see a plain, middle-aged woman standing in front of the information desk. She's wearing a threadbare brown overcoat. In the lapel is a red rose. The soldier smiles and moves toward. He sticks out his right hand to shake while he presents the book to her with his left hand.

"I've been keeping this book for four years with the idea that one day I'd be able to give it to you in person. This is that day. May I have the honor of taking you to dinner?"

The woman seems confused, but in a somber voice, she makes this reply:

"Son, I'm not sure what's going on here, but that lovely young woman you were talking to pulled me aside a few minutes ago and pleaded with me to wear this red rose in my lapel. She said if you still wanted to take me to dinner, she'd be waiting for you in the lobby of the hotel across the street. *She said it was some kind of test....*"

Do You Have What It Takes to Pass the Test?

Did you see that ending coming? I sure didn't.

What do you think would have happened if the soldier had failed to keep his commitment and *given in to temptation* by accepting the lovely woman's invitation? In all likelihood, she would have brushed him off, and he would have lost the opportunity to spend a lifetime with the woman of his dreams.

This story is a perfect analogy for **getting R.E.A.L. and getting rich**. Like the soldier, we all have dreams, whether it's for a "soul mate" or for financial independence and a worry-free retirement. But to live our dreams, we have to pass "some kind of test" by honoring our commitments in the face of many temptations.

If your dream is to **get rich... live rich...** and **retire rich**—and if you *truly* want that dream to become a reality—you will have to pass not one but TWO TESTS—a test for the **Museum Method** and a test for the **Modern Method**.

To pass the test to get rich in four to five decades with the Museum Method, you're going to have to keep your commitment to save and invest, despite daily temptations to spend.

To pass the test to get rich in four to five decades with the **Museum Method**, you're going to have to keep your commitment to save and invest, despite daily *temptations* to spend.

Instead of saving, you'll be tempted to buy that *big-screen TV* you've always wanted.

Instead of investing $4,000 in a tax-deferred IRA, you'll be tempted to spend it on a *family trip to Disney World*.

Instead of continuing to drive the family car after it's paid off and investing the loan payment, you'll be tempted to take out a loan on a *beautiful SUV* you've always wanted (or a *beautiful "fill in the blank"* you've always dreamed about).

But before you give in to those temptations, remind yourself of the payoff if you have the discipline and commitment to resist temptations—**financial freedom and time freedom.**

Passing the Test for the Modern Method

To pass the test and get rich in months and years with the **Modern Method**, you'll be faced with a different set of temptations.

Instead of **opening your mind** to new ways of making money and making a difference in people's lives, you'll be tempted to dismiss a new and different business model because it's "not the way I've always done it."

Instead of doing **R.E.A.L. work** in the evening and weekends to make money and make a new life for yourself and your family, you'll be tempted to relax in front of the TV after doing **real work** building someone else's dream at your nine-to-five day job.

Instead of **doing your due diligence** by finding out more about the **Modern Method**, you'll be tempted to dismiss the opportunity by parroting tired myths, such as "My brother-in-law says these things never work."

Instead of **confronting your fears and making a change** in your life, you'll be tempted to stay in your comfort zone, even if it means being bored and broke.

Instead of **dreaming big dreams** by reaching for the stars in your own business, you'll be tempted to settle for a paycheck that will always leave you with "too much month at the end of the money."

Be Constant, Get Rich

Yes, I know this is tough talk, but before you can **get R.E.A.L. and get rich,** you have to *get real* about what it takes to turn your dreams into reality. The question is, do you have the desire... the drive... and the discipline to hold fast to your commitments TODAY... so that you can enjoy a lifetime of financial security and independence TOMORROW?

The **Millionaire Mindset** is to deny **short-term thrills** so that you don't ever have to worry about **long-term bills.** For that to happen, you need to take the poet John Donne's advice and "be constant."

Be constant in your dreams.

Be constant in your discipline.

And be constant in your daily decisions.

I was constant in applying the **R.E.A.L. principles** discussed in this book. I took the advice of Tom Murphy, my mentor, when he challenged me to change my thinking. I accepted his challenge. I changed my thinking. I changed my habits. I changed my values. And I went from minimum wage... to multi-millionaire.

In closing, I want to thank you for reading my "rags to riches" story.

Now it's time for you to write your own.